FINANCIAL
STATEMENT
ANALYSIS

FINANCIAL STATEMENT ANALYSIS

A Practitioner's Guide

Third Edition

WORKBOOK

Martin Fridson
Fernando Alvarez

JOHN WILEY & SONS, INC.

Published by John Wiley & Sons, Inc., Hoboken, New Jersey.
Published simultaneously in Canada.

This publication is designed to provide accurate and authoritative information in regard to the subject matter covered. It is sold with the understanding that the publisher is not engaged in rendering professional services. If professional advice or other expert assistance is required, the services of a competent professional person should be sought.

Wiley also publishes its books in a variety of electronic formats. Some content that appears in print may not be available in electronic books. For more information about Wiley products visit our Web site at www.wiley.com.

Library of Congress Cataloging-in-Publication Data:

Fridson, Martin S.
  Financial statement analysis : a practitioner's guide, workbook / Martin S. Fridson, Fernando Alvarez.—3rd ed.
    p.   cm.
    ISBN 0-471-40915-4 (cloth : alk. paper)
    ISBN 0-471-40917-0 (university edition)
    ISBN 0-471-40918-9 (workbook)
    ISBN 0-471-40916-2 (Instructor's Guide: Web product)
  1. Financial statements.   2. Ratio analysis.   I. Alvarez, Fernando, 1964–
II. Title.
    HF5681.B2 F772 2002
    657'.3—dc21

                                                    2001007198

Printed in the United States of America.

10   9   8   7   6   5   4   3   2   1

In memory of my father, Harry Yale Fridson, who introduced me to accounting, economics, and logic, as well as the fourth discipline essential to the creation of this book—hard work!

M. F.

For Shari, Virginia, and Armando.

F. A.

ADDITIONAL PRAISE FOR *FINANCIAL STATEMENT ANALYSIS, THIRD EDITION*

"With a solid understanding of accepted accounting standards, one must peel through the fog generated by audited accounting numbers to get a clear picture of any company's financial health. Certainly, Fridson and Alvarez show us how to do just that. What I like best about the book is the authors' ability to provide examples of real-life debacles discussed in the business press that could have been foreseen using the techniques explained in the book and having a healthy dose of skepticism. Their approach to analyzing financial statements should be commended."

—Ivan Brick
Professor and Chair, Finance and Economics Department, Rutgers Business School

"This book should be required reading for the seasoned investor and novice alike. Fridson and Alvarez show, in a very readable format, that diligent analysis still can make a difference. Finally a book that covers not just the basics, but all the subtleties and everything that management doesn't want you to know."

—Robert S. Franklin, CFA
Portfolio Manager, Neuberger Berman, LLC

"Read it, digest it, and review it frequently. Fridson and Alvarez take you through financial statement analysis with many salient examples that expose hidden agendas and help with assessing the true value of securities."

—Ron Habakus
Director of High Yield Investments, Brown Brothers Harriman

"Fridson and Alvarez clearly show why the most successful financial analysts approach their jobs with healthy doses of cynicism. Well written, insightful, and with numerable real life war stories, this book is required reading for all high yield bond analysts at AIG."

—Gordon Massie
Managing Director, High Yield Bonds
American International Group Global Investment Advisors

"Fridson and Alvarez give financial analysts, accountants, investors, auditors and all other finance professionals something to chew over. They succeed in illustrating the use of financial statement analysis with many astonishing real life examples. This book starts where others stop. Clearly, a must read that brings the reader beyond the pure number crunching!"

—Marc J.K. De Ceuster
Professor at the University of Antwerp (Belgium) and Director of Risk Management at Deloitte & Touche

"Alvarez and Fridson have a real gift for expressing the concepts of finance in down-to-earth, understandable ways. The situations they choose, and the skillful way they lay out each example, make all the subtle relationships come to. They are real artists with spreadsheets that are easy for the reader to follow, and easy to adapt to new situations. For instant financial empowerment, buy this book and let Alvarez and Fridson ramp up your financial modeling skills."

—John Edmunds
Director of the Stephen D. Cutler Investment Management Center at Babson College

Preface to Third Edition Workbook

This third edition of *Financial Statement Analysis,* like its predecessors, seeks to equip its readers for practical challenges of contemporary business. Once again, the intention is to acquaint readers who have already acquired basic accounting skills with the complications that arise in applying textbook-derived knowledge to the real world of extending credit and investing in securities. Just as a swiftly changing environment necessitated extensive revisions and additions in the second edition, new concerns and challenges for users of financial statements have accompanied the dawn of the twenty-first century.

For one thing, corporations have shifted their executive compensation plans increasingly toward rewarding senior managers for "enhancing shareholder value." This lofty-sounding concept has a dark side. Chief executive officers who are under growing pressure to boost their corporations' share prices can no longer increase their bonuses by goosing reported earnings through financial reporting tricks that are transparent to the stock market. They must instead devise more insidious methods that gull investors into believing that the reported earnings gains are real. In response to this trend, we have expanded our survey of revenue recognition gimmicks designed to deceive the unwary.

Another innovation that demands increased vigilance by financial analysts is the conversion of stock market proceeds into revenues. In terms of accounting theory, this kind of transformation is the equivalent of alchemy. Companies generate revenue by selling goods or services, not by selling their own shares to the public.

During the Internet stock boom of the late 1990s, however, clever operators found a way around that constraint. Companies took the money they raised in initial public offerings, bought advertising on one another's websites, and recorded the shuttling of dollars as sales. Customers were superfluous to the revenue recognition process. In another variation on the theme, franchisers sold stock, lent the proceeds to franchisees, then immediately had the cash returned under the rubric of fees. By going out for a short stroll and coming back, the proceeds of a financing mutated into revenues.

The artificial nature of these revenues becomes apparent when readers combine an understanding of accounting principles with a corporate finance perspective. We facilitate such integration of disciplines throughout *Financial Statement Analysis,* making excursions into economics and business management as well. In addition, we encourage analysts to consider the institutional context in which financial reporting occurs. Organizational pressures result in divergences from elegant theories, both in the conduct of financial statement analysis and in auditors' interpretations of accounting principles. The issuers of financial statements also exert a strong influence over the creation of the financial principles, with powerful politicians sometimes carrying their water.

A final area in which the new edition offers a sharpened focus involves success stories in the critical examination of financial statements. Wherever we can find the necessary documentation, we show not only how a corporate debacle *could have been* foreseen through application of basis analytical techniques, but how practicing analysts actually did detect the problem before it became widely recognized. Readers will be encouraged by these examples, we hope, to undertake genuine, goal-oriented analysis, instead of simply going through the motions of calculating standard financial ratios. Moreover, the case studies should persuade them to stick to their guns when they spot trouble, despite management's predictable litany. ("Our financial statements are consistent with Generally Accepted Accounting Principles. They have been certified by one of the world's premier auditing firms. We will not allow a band of greedy short-sellers to destroy the value created by our outstanding employees.") Typically, as the vehemence of management's protests increases, conditions deteriorate and accusations of aggressive accounting give way to revelations of fraudulent financial reporting.

The principles and theories put forth in the University Edition of *Financial Statement Analysis, Third Edition,* are reinforced through the questions and exercises in this workbook. Part One, Questions, provides chapter-by-chapter fill-in-the-blank questions, financial statement exercises, and computational exercises. They are designed to be thought-provoking exercises requiring analysis and synthesis of the concepts covered in the book. In short, these are not "regurgitation of information" type questions.

The answers to all questions can be found in Part Two. Answers are provided in ***bold faced, italic type*** in order to facilitate the checking of answers and comprehension of the material.

Financial markets continue to evolve, but certain phenomena appear again and again in new guises. In this vein, companies never lose their resourcefulness in finding new ways to skew perceptions of their performance. By studying their methods closely, analysts can potentially anticipate the variations on old themes that will materialize in years to come.

MARTIN FRIDSON
FERNANDO ALVAREZ

Acknowledgments

Mukesh Agarwal
John Bace
Mitchell Bartlett
Richard Bernstein
Richard Byrne
Richard Cagney
George Chalhoub
Sanford Cohen
Margarita Declet
Sylvan Feldstein
David Fitton
Thomas Flynn III
Daniel Fridson
Igor Fuksman
Ryan Gelrod
Kenneth Goldberg
Susannah Gray
Evelyn Harris
David Hawkins
Avi Katz
Rebecca Keim
James Kenney
Andrew Kroll
Les Levi
Ross Levy
Jennie Ma
Michael Marocco

Eric Matejevich
John Mattis
Pat McConnell
Oleg Melentyev
Krishna Memani
Ann Marie Mullan
Kingman Penniman
Richard Rolnick
Clare Schiedermayer
Gary Schieneman
Bruce Schwartz
Devin Scott
Elaine Sisman
Charles Snow
Vladimir Stadnyk
John Thieroff
Scott Thomas
John Tinker
Kivin Varghese
Sharyl Van Winkle
David Waill
Steven Waite
Douglas Watson
Burton Weinstein
Stephen Weiss
David Whitcomb
Mark Zand

Contents

PART ONE

Questions

QUESTIONS ON EACH CHAPTER

Chapter 1: The Adversarial Nature of Financial Reporting

1. Three ways that corporations can use financial reporting to enhance their value are:

   a. _____

   b. _____

   c. _____

2. Corporations routinely _____ because the appearance of _____ receives a higher _____ multiple.

3. The following are some of the powerful limitations to continued growth faced by companies:

   a. _____

   b. _____

   c. _____

4. _____ reached its zenith of popularity during the _____ movement of the 1960s. However, by the 1980s, the stock market had converted the _____ into a _____ .

5. The surprise element in Manville Corporation's 1982 bankruptcy was, in part, a function of _____ .

6. Some of the stories used to sell stocks to individual investors are:

   a. _____

   b. A "play" in some current economic trend such as

      i. _____

      ii. _____

   c. _____

7. The ostensible purpose of financial reporting is _____ of a corporation's earnings.

8. Over a two-year period, BGT paid L&H $35 million to develop translation software. L&H then bought BGT and the translation product along with it. The net effect was that instead _____ , _____ , L&H recognized _____ .

Chapter 2: The Balance Sheet

1, A study conducted on behalf of Big Five accounting firm Arthur Andersen showed that between _____ and _____ , book value fell from _____% to _____% of the stock market value of public companies in the United States.

2. In the examples above, there is no accounting event because _____ .

3. As in the case of _____ , the historical cost principle makes comparable companies appear quite dissimilar. The equally large _____ of another company with low-cost debt will not be reflected on its balance sheet, simply because _____ .

4. Through stock-for-stock acquisitions, the sharp rise in equity prices during the late 1990s was transformed into _____, despite the usual assumption that _____ .

5. A reasonable estimate of a low-profit company's true equity value would be _____ .

6. Determining the cost of capital is a notoriously controversial subject in the financial field, complicated by _____ and _____ .

7. Instead of striving for theoretical purity on the matter, analysts should adopt a _____, using the measure of equity value _____ .

8. Users of financial statements can process only _____, and they do not always have _____ .

9. Where feasible, users of financial statements should also solicit as _____ regarding risks not spelled out _____ .

Chapter 3 The Income Statement

1. Students of financial statements must keep up with _____ of the past few years in transforming _____ into _____ .

2. Besides facilitating comparisons between a company's present and past results, the _____ can highlight important facts _____ .

3. The more widely diversified pharmaceutical manufacturers can be expected to have _____ percentage _____, as well as _____ percentage _____ expenses, than industry peers that focus exclusively on _____ .

4. Executives whose bonuses rise _____ have a strong in-centive not only _____, but also to use _____ .

5. Along with _____ , another major expense category that can be controlled through _____ is _____ .

6. A company knows that creating _____ expectations about _____ can raise _____ and lower _____ .

7. An extraordinary item is reported on an _____ basis, below the _____ from continuing operations.

8. In recent years, _____ has become a catchall for charges that companies wish analysts to consider _____ , but which do not qualify for _____ .

9. The most dangerous trap that users of financial statements must avoid walking into, however, is inferring that the term *restructuring* connotes _____ .

10. The purpose of providing pro forma results was to help analysts _____ accurately when some event caused _____ to convey a misleading impression.

11. Computer software producers got into the act by _____ from the expenses considered in calculating _____ .

12. In fact, analysts who hope to forecast future financial results accurately *must* apply _____ and set aside genuinely _____ .

13. An older, but not obsolete, device for beefing up reported income is _____ .

14. A corporation can easily accelerate its sales growth by _____ and _____ . Creating genuine value for shareholders though is more difficult, although unwary investors sometimes fail to recognize the distinction.

15. If Company A generates external growth by acquiring Company B and neither Company A nor its new subsidiary increases

its profitability, then _____ the merged companies
is _____ than the sum of the two companies' values.

16. As synergies go, projections of economies of scale in combinations of companies _____ tend to be more plausible than economies of scope purportedly available to companies in _____ businesses.

17. Professor Beneish's statistical analysis shows that the presence of the following factors increases the probability of earnings manipulation:

a. _____

b. _____

c. _____

d. _____

Chapter 4: The Statement of Cash Flows

1. For financial reporting (as opposed to _____) purposes, a publicly owned company generally seeks to maximize _____, which investors use as a basis for valuing its shares.

2. In a classic LBO, a group of investors acquires a business by _____ and _____ the balance.

3. Analysts evaluating the investment merits of the LBO proposal would miss the point if they focused on _____ rather than _____.

4. The essential idea of a _____ is to acquire a business with a sliver of equity and a large amount of _____, and then pay off the debt with _____.

5. The EBITDA multiple may come down because _____ perceive that the LBO organizers _____ on capital spending during their stewardship, meaning that _____ will be required going forward.

6. The _____, rather than the _____, provides the best information about a highly leveraged firm's financial health.

7. Revenues build gradually during the _____ phase, when the company is just _____ and _____. Growth and profits accelerate rapidly during the _____ phase, as the company's products begin to penetrate the market and the _____. During the _____ period, growth in sales and earnings decelerates as the _____. In the _____ phase, sales opportunities are limited to the replacement of products previously sold, plus _____. Price competition often intensifies at this stage, as companies _____. The _____ stage does not automatically follow maturity, but over long periods some industries do get swept away by _____. Sharply declining sales and earnings, ultimately resulting in _____, characterize industries in decline.

8. _____ are start-ups that survive long enough to reach the stage of entering the public market.

9. _____, are past the cash strain faced by growth companies that must fund large _____ programs.

10. By studying the cash flow statement, an analyst can make informed judgments on such questions as:

    a. _____

    b. _____

    c. _____

11. If corporation's financial strain becomes acute, the board of directors may take the comparatively extreme step of _____.

12. A company with a strong balance sheet can fund much of that cash need by increasing its _____ (credit extended by vendors). External financing may be needed, however, if accumulation of unsold goods causes _____ to rise disproportionately to _____. Similarly, if customers begin paying more slowly than formerly, _____ can widen the gap between _____ and _____.

13. Overinvestment has unquestionably led, in many industries, to prolonged periods of _____, producing in turn chronically _____. In retrospect, the firms involved would have served their shareholders better if they had _____ or _____, instead of _____.

14. Another less obvious risk of eschewing financial flexibility is the danger of permanently losing _____ through _____ occasioned by recessions.

15. The cash flow statement is the best tool for measuring _____, which, contrary to a widely held view, is not merely a security blanket for _____. In the hands of an aggressive but prudent management, a cash flow cushion can enable a company to _____ when competitors are forced to cut back.

Chapter 5: What Is Profit?

1. Profitability is a yardstick by which businesspeople can measure their _____ and justify _____.

2. When calculating _____ profits, the analyst must take care to consider only genuine revenues and deduct all relevant costs.

3. There can be no bona fide profit without _____. Bona fide profits are the only kind of profits _____ in financial analysis.

4. Merely _____, it is clear, does not increase wealth.

5. An essential element of genuinely useful financial statement analysis is: _____.

6. The issuer of the statements can _____ or _____ its reported earnings simply by using its latitude to assume shorter or longer _____.

7. The rate at which the tax code allows owners to write off property overstates _____.

8. In the _____, companies typically record depreciation and amortization expense that far exceeds physical wear-and-tear on assets.

9. In many industries, fixed assets consist mainly of _____. The major risk of analytical error does not arise from the possibility that _____, but the reverse.

Chapter 6: Revenue Recognition

1. Many corporations employ _____ practices that comply with GAAP yet _____.

2. Analysts were questioning Informix's _____; in particular, when Informix revealed that about $170 million of its 1996 sales to computer makers and _____ represented _____ that had not yet been _____.

3. Some of the reasons software manufacturers defer recognition of revenue are:

a. _____

b. _____

c. _____

d. _____

4. Agreements with resellers that:

a. _____

b. _____

c. _____

d. _____

mean that license revenue from these transactions should not be recorded _____; rather it should instead be recorded at the time _____.

5. The Informix affair teaches analysts not to construe _____ as an assurance of integrity in financial reporting. _____ reporting differs from fraudulent reporting, in a _____, but a corporate culture that embraces the former can foster the latter.

6. Staying alert to evidence of flawed, _____, reporting is essential, even when the auditors _____.

7. In 1994, KnowledgeWare began supplementing its own sales-force's efforts with agreements _____. Almost immediately, the company started to encounter difficulties in _____. In restating the results, management said that it had booked as revenues _____.

8. The receivables-related bombshell that KnowledgeWare dropped on August 30, 1994, was telegraphed by _____ in

KnowledgeWare's 10Q for the first fiscal quarter, received by the SEC way back on November 2, 1993.

9. Prior to the change in accounting practice, which FAS 101 made mandatory, Wal-Mart booked layaway sales _____. Under the new and more conservative method, the company began to recognize the sales _____ .

10. As in any sales situation, aggressive pursuit of new business could result in _____. On average, the newer members might prove to be _____ or less committed to physical fitness than _____ .

11. Under GAAP, the general requirement was to spread membership fees _____. If a company offered refunds, it could not _____ until the refund period expired, unless there was _____ to enable management to estimate _____ with reasonable confidence.

12. GAAP addresses the problem through the _____, which permits the company to recognize revenue in _____, rather than in line with its billing.

13. The SEC claimed that to inflate revenues and profits, management at Sequoia Systems:

    a. _____

    b. _____

    c. _____

14. Loading the distribution channels consists of _____ to accept larger shipments of goods than _____ .

15. Inevitably, the underlying trend of final sales to consumers slows down, at least temporarily. At that point, the manufacturer's growth in reported revenue will maintain its trend only _____ , relative to their sales. If the distributors balk,

_____, forcing a _____ of previously recorded profits.

16. Users of financial statements should not be intimidated by corporate _____ that denounce allegedly irresponsible _____.

17. A stock's value is a function of expected _____, which partly depend on the _____ vis-à-vis its competitors'.

18. Analysts who strive to go beyond routine _____ can profit by seeking _____ of corporate disclosure, even when _____ have already placed _____.

19. Grace executives reckoned that with earnings already meeting Wall Street analysts' forecasts, a windfall _____ the company's stock price. Such an inference would have been consistent with investors' customary _____ that they perceive to be generated by _____.

20. According to Michael Jensen: "Tell a manager that he will get a bonus when targets are realized and two things will happen":

    a. _____

    b. _____

21. According to Jensen, almost every company uses a budget system that _____ employees for _____ and punishes them _____. He proposes reforming the system by severing the link between _____ and _____.

Chapter 7: Expense Recognition

1. Corporate managers are just as creative _____ and _____ the recognition of _____ as they are in maximizing and speeding up the _____.

2. To attract subscribers, AOL mailed millions of solicitations and, through arrangements with computer manufacturers, gave away free trial subscriptions. The company did not _____. Instead, AOL _____, and then _____ over periods of 12 to 18 months.

3. AOL precipitated the plunge in its share prices by cutting the price of its online service by 63%. The move represented _____, as well as to the migration of _____, where most information and entertainment was offered to subscribers _____.

4. Repeating a recurrent theme in the annals of financial reporting controversies, AOL had initially managed to _____, to which investors duly assigned _____, by exploiting the not _____ of a new industry _____.

5. During 1999, Chairman Louis Gerstner hailed IBM's _____ as a key to its recent earnings improvement.

6. The investigating accountants and lawyers interviewed more than 200 suppliers of Wickes PLC to determine how many _____. Clearly, outside analysts, working only with _____, could not have pieced together all of the details of the scheme.

7. Rudimentary analysis of Oxford's financial statements provided more than a hint of _____. Consider the Form 10-Q report for the quarter ended June 30, 1997, the last filed by the company before the October bloodbath. The _____ displayed the classic problem that first gave rise to _____. Even though _____ for 1997's first half rose by 74.6% over the comparable 1996 period, _____ deteriorated to −$107.3 million from $139.2 million. The bulk of that adverse swing resulted from medical costs payable turning from a large _____ to a major _____.

Chapter 8: The Applications and Limitations of EBITDA

1. The impetus for trying to redirect investors' focus to _____ or other variants has been _____ recorded by many "new economy" companies.

2. Users of financial statements had discovered certain limitations in net income as a _____. They observed that two companies in the same industry could report similar _____, yet have substantially different _____.

3. Net income is not, to the disappointment of analysts, a standard by which every company's _____ can be compared.

4. The accounting standards leave companies considerable discretion regarding the _____ they assign to their _____. The same applies to amortization schedules for _____.

5. For some companies, the sum of net income, income taxes, and interest expense is not equivalent to EBIT, reflecting the presence of such factors as _____ below _____.

6. Shifting investors' attention away from traditional fixed-charge coverage and toward _____ was particularly beneficial during the 1980s, when some buyouts were so _____ that _____ would not cover pro forma interest expense even in a good year.

7. Capital spending is likely to exceed depreciation over time as the company _____ to accommodate _____. Another reason that capital spending may run higher than depreciation is that newly acquired equipment may be _____ than the old equipment being written off, as a function of _____.

8. Delaying equipment purchases and repairs that are _____ but not _____, should inflict no lasting damage on the

company's _____ provided the _____ lasts for only a few quarters.

9. Depreciation is not available as a long-run source of cash for _____ . This was a lesson applicable not only to the extremely _____ deals of the 1980s, but also to the more _____ capitalized transactions of later years.

10. Beaver's definition of cash flow was more stringent than _____ since he did not add back either _____ or _____ to net income.

11. Beaver did not conclude that analysts should rely solely on the _____ , but merely that it was the single best _____ .

12. Some investment managers consider that the single ratio of _____ (as they define it) to _____ predicts bankruptcy better than all of _____ quantitative and qualitative considerations combined.

13. Aside from _____ , the amount of working capital needed to run a business represents a fairly constant _____ of a company's sales. Therefore, if inventories or receivables _____ materially as a percentage of sales, analysts should strongly suspect that the earnings are _____ , even though management will invariably offer a _____ explanation.

14. If a company resorts to stretching out its payables, two other ratios that will send out warning signals are:

    a. _____

    b. _____

15. Merrill Lynch investment strategist Richard Bernstein points out that _____ earnings tend to be more stable than _____ earnings, EBIT tends to be more stable than

_____ earnings, and _____ tends to be more stable than EBIT.

16. Strategist Bernstein found that by attempting to _____ inherent in companies' earnings, investors reduced the _____ of their stock selection.

Chapter 9: The Reliability of Disclosure and Audits

1. Fear of the consequences of breaking the law keep corporate managers in line. _____ the law is another matter, though, in the minds of many executives. If their bonuses depend on _____, they can usually see their way clear to adopting that course.

2. At some point, _____ becomes a moral imperative, but in the real world, accounting firms must be _____.

3. _____ is an unambiguous violation of accounting standards, but audits do not _____.

4. When challenged on inconsistencies in their numbers, companies sometimes _____, rather than any intention to _____.

5. According to president and chief executive of Trump World's Fair Casino Hotel, the firm's focus in 1999 was threefold:

   a. _____

   b. _____

   c. _____

6. One source of Sunbeam's supposedly robust 1997 profits, according to the accounting firm that the company's board hired for the review, was an _____ in 1996.

7. Deidra DenDanto, formerly of the accounting firm of _____, stated in a memo (which unfortunately never reached the board of Sunbeam) that booking _____ as sales was _____.

8. Abundant evidence has emerged over the years of corporate managers _____ to paint as rosy a picture as possible.

9. According to Wade Meyercord, an outside director of California Micro Devices, who helped to uncover the fraud and took over as chairman, the fakery included _____.

10. In theory, the _____ committee of the board of directors serves as _____ in the struggle for _____.

11. Many companies are either _____ or _____. Rather than laying down the law (or GAAP), the auditors typically wind up _____ to arrive at a point where they can convince themselves that _____ have been satisfied.

Chapter 10: Mergers-and-Acquisitions Accounting

1. Choosing a method of accounting for a merger or acquisition does not affect the combined companies' subsequent _____ or _____. The discretionary accounting choices can have a _____, however, on _____.

2. Amortization of goodwill entails _____. Neither does it generate cash _____, because it is not _____. The amortization does reduce _____.

3. From a cash flow standpoint, investors are actually better off under the _____ method.

4. There are approximately 10 academic studies of the issue, covering periods from the 1960s to the 1990s. The studies consistently found that the _____ reported earnings generated

by _____ did not cause the stocks of the acquiring companies' to outperform the stocks of companies employing _____.

5. Among technology companies, a popular way to boost earnings in the pooling-of-interests era involved _____ of acquired companies.

6. For example, one M&A-related gambit entails the GAAP-sanctioned use, for financial reporting purposes, of _____. Typically, companies use this discretion to simplify the closing of their books at month- or quarter-end.

7. There can be no guarantee of loans secured by stock issued in the combination, which would effectively _____ implicit in a bona fide _____. _____ of stock and _____ are likewise prohibited.

Chapter 11: Profits in Pensions

1. Under SFAS No. 87, "Accounting for Pensions," the investment returns on a corporate pension plan's investment portfolio flows into _____. Management can elect to _____ or a portion of the year's net pension benefit (cost) as part of _____ and then run it through _____. Alternatively, the company can recognize the pension-related income by reducing _____.

2. When projecting IBM's future earnings, it is important to segregate _____ from _____. Otherwise, the analysis will give management _____ for a general _____.

3. Analysts should also note that the accounting rules for pension income allow management, within certain bounds, to _____ from the _____ to the _____.

4. In principle, one would expect a company to base its assumption on _____ .

5. Management cannot invariably modulate their impact on reported earnings as desired. Among the effects is_____ that may arise from _____ . Such events may be large enough to _____ .

Chapter 12: Forecasting Financial Statements

1. It is _____ that determine the value of a company's stock and the _____ that determines credit quality.

2. The process of financial projections is an extension of _____ and _____ , based on assumptions about future _____ , _____ , and _____ .

3. Sales projections for the company's business can be developed with the help of such sources as _____ , _____ , and firms that sell _____ models.

4. Basic industries such as _____ , _____ , and _____ tend to lend themselves best to the _____ described here. In technology-driven industries and "hits-driven" businesses such as _____ and _____ , the connection between _____ and the _____ will tend to be looser.

5. The expected intensity of industry competition, which affects a company's _____ on to customers or to retain _____ , influences the _____ forecast.

6. Since the segment information may show only operating income, and not _____ , the analyst must add _____ to operating income, then make assumptions about the allocation of _____ and _____ expense by segment.

7. The R&D percentage may change if, for example, the company _____ in an industry that is either significantly more, or significantly less, _____ than its existing operations.

8. The key to the forecasting interest expense method employed here is to estimate the firm's embedded cost of debt, that is, the _____ on the company's _____.

9. Accurately projecting interest expense for _____ companies is important because _____ may depend on the size of _____ they must cover each quarter.

10. The completed income statement projection supplies _____ of the projected statement of cash flows.

11. Before assuming a constant-percentage relationship, the analyst must verify that _____.

12. A sizable _____ might be presumed to be directed toward share repurchase, reducing _____, if management has indicated a desire to _____ and is _____ by its board of directors.

13. Typically, the analyst must modify the underlying _____ assumptions, and therefore the projections, several times during the year as _____ diverges from _____.

14. A firm may have considerable room to cut _____ in the short run if it suffers a decline in funds provided by _____. A projection that ignored this _____ could prove overly pessimistic.

15. An interest rate decline will have limited impact on a company for which interest costs represent a _____. The impact will be greater on a company with a large interest cost component and with much of its debt at _____. This assumes the return on the company's assets is _____.

16. Analysts are generally not arrogant enough to try to forecast the figures accurately to the first decimal place, that is, to the _____ for a company with revenues in the _____.

17. It is generally inappropriate to compare a _____ item (EBITDA) with a balance sheet figure, especially in the case of a _____ company.

18. It is unwise to base an investment decision on historical statements that antedate a major financial change such as:

    a. _____

    b. _____

    c. _____

    d. _____

19. A pro forma income statement for a single year provides no information about _____ in sales and earnings of _____ that is being spun off.

20. Pro forma adjustments for a divestment do not capture the potential benefits of increased _____ on the company's _____.

21. The earnings shown in a merger-related pro forma income statement may be higher than the company can sustain because:
    a. The acquired company's owners may be shrewdly selling out at top dollar, anticipating a _____ that is foreseeable by _____, but not to the acquiring corporation's management.
    b. Mergers of companies in the same industry often work out poorly due to _____.
    c. Inappropriately applying _____ to an industry with very different requirements.

22. A _____ investor buying a 30-year bond is certainly interested in the issuer's financial prospects beyond _____. Similarly, a substantial percentage of the present value of future dividends represented by a stock's price lies _____ .

23. Radical financial restructurings such as _____, _____, and _____ necessitate _____ projections.

24. Of the various types of analysis of financial statements, projecting _____ and requires the greatest skill and produces _____ .

25. The lack of _____ is what makes financial forecasting so _____. When betting huge sums in the face of _____, it is essential that investors understand _____ as fully as they possibly can.

Chapter 13: Credit Analysis

1. Financial statements tell much about a borrower's _____ to repay a loan, but disclose little about the equally important _____ to repay.

2. If a company is dependent on raw materials provided by a subsidiary, there may be a _____ presumption that it will stand behind the subsidiary's _____, even _____ .

3. Illiquidity manifests itself as an excess of current _____, over _____. The _____ ratio gauges the risk of this occurring by comparing the claims against the company that will become payable during _____ with the assets that are already in the form of cash or that will be converted to cash during _____ .

4. The greater the amount by which asset values could deteriorate, the greater the _____, and the greater the creditor's

sense of _____. Equity is by definition _____ minus
_____.

5. Aggressive _____ frequently try to satisfy the letter of a
   _____ leverage limit imposed by lenders, without fulfilling the _____ behind it.

6. A firm that "zeros out" its _____ at some point in each
   operating cycle can legitimately argue that its "true" leverage is
   represented by the _____ on its balance sheet.

7. Current maturities of long-term debt should enter into the calculation of _____, based on a conservative assumption that the company will replace maturing debt with
   _____.

8. Exposure to interest rate fluctuations can also arise from long-
   term _____. Companies can limit this risk by using
   _____.

9. Public financial statements typically provide _____ information about the extent to which the issuer has _____
   its exposure to interest rate fluctuations through _____.

10. Analysts should remember that the ultimate objective is not to
    _____ but to _____.

11. In general, the credit analyst must recognize the heightened
    level of risk implied by the presence of preferred stock in
    the _____. One formal way to take this risk into
    account is to calculate the ratio of _____ to
    _____.

12. In addition to including capital leases in the total debt calcula-
    tion, analysts should also take into account the _____ li-
    abilities represented by contractual payments on _____,
    which are reported as _____ in the _____ to Fi-
    nancial Statements.

13. A corporation can employ leverage yet avoid showing debt on its consolidated balance sheet by _____ or forming _____ .

14. Under SFAS _____ , balance sheet recognition is now given to pension liabilities related to employees' service to date. Similarly, SFAS _____ requires recognition of postretirement health care benefits as an on-balance sheet liability.

15. The precise formula for _____ a ratio is less important than the assurance that it is _____ for all companies being evaluated.

16. In general, credit analysts should assume that the achievement of _____ bond ratings is a _____ goal of corporate management.

17. The contemporary view is that profits are ultimately what sustain _____ and _____ . High profits keep plenty of cash flowing through the system and confirm the value of productive assets such as _____ and _____ .

18. The cumulative effect of a change in accounting procedures will appear _____ or after _____ have already been deducted. The sum of net income and provision for income taxes will then differ from the _____ that appears in the income statement.

19. Operating margin shows how well management has run the business _____ wisely, controlling _____ before taking into account financial policies, which largely determine _____ , and _____ , which is outside management's control.

20. Fixed-charge coverage is an _____ ratio of major interest to credit analysts. It measures the ability of a company's _____ to meet the _____ on its debt, the lender's most direct concern. In its simplest form, the fixed-charge

coverage ratio indicates the _____ by which _____ suffice to pay _____ .

21. Regardless of whether it is _____ or _____, however, all interest accrued must be covered by _____ and should therefore appear in the _____ of the fixed-charge coverage calculation.

22. The two complications that arise in connection with incorporating operating lease payments into the fixed-charge coverage calculation are:

   a. _____

   b. _____

23. Companies sometimes argue that the denominator of the fixed-charge coverage ratio should include only _____ expense, that is, the difference between _____ and income derived from _____, generally consisting of marketable securities.

24. Ratios related to sources and uses of funds measure credit quality at the most elemental level—a company's ability to _____ .

25. Given corporations' general reluctance to sell new equity, a recurrent cash shortfall is likely to be made up with _____ financing, leading to a rise in _____ ratio.

26. A company that suffers a prolonged downtrend in its ratio of _____ is likely to get more deeply into debt, and therefore become _____ with each succeeding year.

27. Unlike earnings, _____ is essentially a programmed item, a cash flow assured by the accounting rules. The higher the percentage of cash flow derived from _____, the higher is the _____ of a company's cash flow, and the _____ its financial flexibility on the vagaries of the marketplace.

28. Analysts cannot necessarily assume that all is well simply because capital expenditures consistently exceed depreciation. Among the issues to consider are:

    a. _____

    b. _____

    c. _____

    d. _____

29. A limitation of combination ratios that incorporate balance-sheet figures is that they have little meaning if _____.

30. The underlying notion of a turnover ratio is that a company requires a certain level of _____ and _____ to support a given volume of sales.

31. A _____ is a possible explanation of declining inventory turnover. In this case, the inventory may not have suffered a severe reduction in value, but there are nevertheless unfavorable implications for _____. Until the inventory glut can be worked off by _____ to match the lower _____, the company may have to borrow to finance its unusually high working capital, thereby increasing its _____.

32. Fixed-charge coverage, too, has a weakness, for it is based on _____, which are subject to considerable manipulation.

33. Built from two comparatively hard numbers, the ratio of to _____ provides one of the best single measures of _____.

34. Expected _____ have an important bearing on the decision to _____ or _____ credit, as well as on the of debt securities.

35. Line of business is another basis for defining _____.

36. Beyond a certain point, calculating and comparing companies on the basis of _____ financial ratios contributes little _____ .

37. _____ or _____ financial ratios can have different implications for different companies.

38. Quantitative models such as Zeta, as well as others that have been devised using various mathematical techniques, have several distinct benefits such as:

    a. _____

    b. _____

    c. _____

39. Like the quantitative models consisting of _____ , the default risk models based on stock prices provide useful, but _____ , signals.

Chapter 14: Equity Analysis

1. In this chapter, the discussion focuses primarily on the use of financial statements in _____ .

2. Of the methods of fundamental common stock analysis, no other approach matches the intuitive appeal of regarding the stock price as the _____ of expected _____ dividends. This approach is analogous to the _____ calculation for a bond and therefore facilitates the comparison of different _____ of a single _____ .

3. By thinking through the logic of the _____ method, the analyst will find that value always comes back to _____ .

4. The company's earnings growth rate may diverge from its sales growth due to changes in its _____ .

5. As a rule, a _____ company will not increase its dividend on a regular, annual basis.

6. Many analysts argue that _____, rather than _____, is the true determinant of dividend-paying capability.

7. Cash generated from _____, which is generally more difficult for companies to manipulate than _____, can legitimately be viewed as the preferred measure of future _____.

8. The ability to vary the _____, and therefore to assign a _____ or _____ multiple to a company's earnings, is the equity analyst's defense against earnings _____ by management.

9. It is appropriate to assign an _____ discount factor to the earnings of a company that competes against larger, better-capitalized firms. A small company _____ of depth in management and concentration of _____.

10. A building-materials manufacturer may claim to be cushioned against fluctuations in housing starts because of a strong emphasis in its product line on _____ .

11. Analysts should be especially wary of companies that have tended to jump on the bandwagon of _____ associated with the _____ of the moment.

12. Earnings per share will not grow merely because _____ .

13. Leverage reaches a limit, since lenders will not continue advancing funds beyond a certain point as _____ .

14. One way to increase earnings per share is to _____ .

15. To the extent that the company funds share buybacks with idle cash, the increase in _____ is offset by a reduction arising from _____ .

16. Like most ratio analysis, the Du Pont Formula is valuable not only for _____ but also for _____ .

17. Besides introducing greater volatility into the _____, adding debt to the balance sheet demonstrates _____ .

18. Some companies have the potential to raise their share prices by _____, while others can increase their value by _____ .

19. Management's main adversaries in battles over _____ were aggressive _____ .

20. At least in the early stages, before some raiders became overly aggressive in their financial forecast assumptions, it was feasible to extract value without creating undue bankruptcy risk, simply by _____ .

21. In future bear markets, when stocks again sell at depressed price-earnings multiples, investors will probably renew their focus on _____ .

22. A leveraged buyout can bring about improved profitability for either of two reasons:

    a. _____

    b. _____

23. Today's _____ may be a precursor of tomorrow's bankruptcy by a company that has economized its way to _____ .

24. A focus on _____ multiples, the best-known form of fundamental analysis, is not the investor's _____ to relying on technicians' stock charts.

25. For the investor who takes a longer view, _____ provides an invaluable reference point for valuation.

FINANCIAL STATEMENT EXERCISES

1. Indicate in which of the principal financial statements each item appears.

   a.

Item	Balance Sheet	Income Statement	Statement of Cash Flows
Accounts Payable			
Accumulated Depreciation			
Adjusted Net Income			
Capital Expenditures			
Cash and Equivalents—Change			
Common Shares Outstanding			
Current Debt—Changes			
Direct Operating Activities			
Earnings per Share (Fully Diluted)			
Earnings per Share (Primary)			
Equity in Net Loss (Earnings)			
Extraordinary Items			
Financing Activities—Net Cash Flow			
Gross Plant, Property, and Equipment			
Income before Extraordinary Items			
Indirect Operating Activities			
Interest Paid—Net			
Investing Activities			
Investment Tax Credit			
Long-Term Debt Due In One Year			
Minority Interest			
Net Receivables			
Operating Activities—Net Cash Flow			
Other Assets and Liabilities—Net Change			
Other Investments			
Preferred Stock—Nonredeemable			
Pretax Income			
Retained Earnings			
Sale of Property, Plant, and Equipment			
Selling, General, and Administrative Expense			
Stock Equivalents			
Total Current Assets			
Total Income Taxes			
Total Preferred Stock			

b.

Item	Balance Sheet	Income Statement	Statement of Cash Flows
Accrued Expenses			
Adjusted Available for Common			
Available for Common			
Cash and Equivalents			
Common Equity			
Cost of Goods Sold			
Deferred Taxes			
Dividends per Share			
Earnings per Share (Primary)			
Equity			
Financing Activities			
Funds from Operations—Other			
Income Taxes Paid			
Interest Expense			
Inventory—Decrease (Increase)			
Investing Activities—Other			
Investments at Equity			
Long-Term Debt			
Long-Term Debt—Reduction			
Net Plant, Property, and Equipment			
Notes Payable			
Other Assets			
Other Current Liabilities			
Preferred Dividends			
Prepaid Expenses			
Receivables—Decrease (Increase)			
Sale of Investments			
Savings Due to Common			
Special Items			
Total Assets			
Total Equity			
Total Liabilities and Equity			

C.

Item	Balance Sheet	Income Statement	Statement of Cash Flows
Accounts Payable and Accrued Liabilities— Increase (Decrease)			
Acquisitions			
Assets			
Capital Surplus			
Cash Dividends			
Common Stock			
Deferred Charges			
Discontinued Operations			
Earnings per Share (Fully Diluted)			
EPS from Operations			
Exchange Rate Effect			
Financing Activities—Other			
Gross Profit			
Income Taxes—Accrued—Increase (Decrease)			
Intangibles			
Inventories			
Investing Activities—Net Cash Flow			
Investments—Increase			
Liabilities			
Long-Term Debt—Issuance			
Minority Interest			
Non-Operating Income/Expense			
Operating Profit			
Other Current Assets			
Other Liabilities			
Preferred Stock—Redeemable			
Purchase of Common and Preferred Stock			
Sale of Common and Preferred Stock			
Sales			
Short-Term Investments—Change			
Taxes Payable			
Total Current Liabilities			
Total Liabilities			
Treasury Stock			

2.　Construct common form balance sheets from the balance sheets of the following firms, determine their operating strategies, and discuss the implications.

　　a.　Coors

Annual Balance Sheet **($ Millions)**	**Dec00**	**Dec99**	**Dec98**	**Dec97**	**Dec96**
ASSETS					
Cash and Equivalents	192.520	276.993	256.228	211.038	110.905
Net Receivables	127.078	159.660	126.609	124.485	114.343
Inventories	109.924	107.257	102.660	106.479	121.070
Other Current Assets	68.229	68.911	63.494	75.192	70.324
Total Current Assets	497.751	612.821	548.991	517.194	416.642
Gross Plant, Property, and Equipment	2,432.750	2,328.568	2,229.723	2,144.937	2,127.811
Accumulated Depreciation	1,696.957	1,614.567	1,515.282	1,411.820	1,313.709
Net Plant, Property, and Equipment	735.793	714.001	714.441	733.117	814.102
Investments at Equity	56.300	69.200	62.300	51.700	47.600
Other Investments	193.675	2.890	31.444	47.100	0.000
Intangibles	29.446	31.292	23.114	22.880	21.374
Other Assets	116.339	116.172	80.308	40.092	62.818
TOTAL ASSETS	1,629.304	1,546.376	1,460.598	1,412.083	1,362.536
LIABILITIES					
Long-Term Debt Due in One Year	0.000	0.000	40.000	27.500	17.000
Accounts Payable	186.105	155.344	132.193	113.864	110.696
Taxes Payable	0.000	8.439	10.130	13.660	8.983
Other Current Liabilities	193.231	228.921	201.589	204.122	155.769
Total Current Liabilities	379.336	392.704	383.912	359.146	292.448
Long-Term Debt	105.000	105.000	105.000	145.000	176.000
Deferred Taxes	89.986	78.733	65.779	76.219	76.083
Investment Tax Credit	0.000	0.000	0.000	0.000	0.000
Other Liabilities	122.593	128.400	131.109	95.150	102.518
EQUITY					
Common Stock	9.801	9.703	9.688	9.736	9.989
Capital Surplus	11.203	5.773	10.505	0.000	31.436
Retained Earnings	911.385	826.063	754.605	726.832	674.062
Common Equity	932.389	841.539	774.798	736.568	715.487
TOTAL EQUITY	932.389	841.539	774.798	736.568	715.487
TOTAL LIABILITIES AND EQUITY	1,629.304	1,546.376	1,460.598	1,412.083	1,362.536
COMMON SHARES OUTSTANDING	37.131	36.722	36.655	36.859	37.922

b. Genesee

Annual Balance Sheet ($ Millions)	Apr01	Apr00	Apr99	Apr98	Apr97
ASSETS					
Cash and Equivalents	21.274	15.678	13.800	20.500	37.148
Net Receivables	3.471	2.776	10.222	10.163	11.037
Inventories	8.758	9.197	16.414	14.258	13.957
Other Current Assets	5.697	0.174	1.148	1.998	1.979
Total Current Assets	39.200	27.825	41.584	46.919	64.121
Gross Plant, Property, and Equipment	17.917	17.201	125.206	117.911	112.033
Accumulated Depreciation	5.680	4.572	88.166	84.600	79.047
Net Plant, Property, and Equipment	12.237	12.629	37.040	33.311	32.986
Investments at Equity	0.000	0.000	5.343	5.534	4.949
Other Investments	10.229	0.000	28.285	34.638	32.144
Intangibles	25.426	26.662	28.280	10.737	0.000
Other Assets	2.910	28.655	3.421	4.450	2.729
TOTAL ASSETS	90.002	95.771	143.953	135.589	136.929
LIABILITIES					
Long-Term Debt Due in One Year	1.474	0.300	0.082	0.000	0.000
Notes Payable	0.000	0.000	3.000	0.000	0.000
Accounts Payable	1.281	1.454	8.421	8.358	9.611
Taxes Payable	0.000	0.064	1.215	0.692	0.932
Other Current Liabilities	1.468	3.746	10.964	9.011	8.424
Total Current Liabilities	4.223	5.564	23.682	18.061	18.967
Long-Term Debt	4.499	5.973	4.679	0.000	0.000
Deferred Taxes	0.000	0.381	8.251	9.295	8.789
Minority Interest	0.000	0.000	2.479	2.227	1.690
Other Liabilities	11.947	0.646	15.825	15.886	15.928
EQUITY					
Common Stock	0.858	0.858	0.858	0.858	0.858
Capital Surplus	5.392	5.847	5.856	5.842	5.834
Retained Earnings	64.576	79.903	85.769	86.895	88.368
Less: Treasury Stock	1.493	3.401	3.446	3.475	3.505
Common Equity	69.333	83.207	89.037	90.120	91.555
TOTAL EQUITY	69.333	83.207	89.037	90.120	91.555
TOTAL LIABILITIES AND EQUITY	90.002	95.771	143.953	135.589	136.929
COMMON SHARES OUTSTANDING	1.674	1.620	1.619	1.618	1.617

c. Red Hook

Annual Balance Sheet **($ Millions)**	**Apr01**	**Apr00**	**Apr99**	**Apr98**	**Apr97**
ASSETS					
Cash and Equivalents	21.274	15.678	13.800	20.500	37.148
Net Receivables	3.471	2.776	10.222	10.163	11.037
Inventories	8.758	9.197	16.414	14.258	13.957
Other Current Assets	5.697	0.174	1.148	1.998	1.979
Total Current Assets	39.200	27.825	41.584	46.919	64.121
Gross Plant, Property, and Equipment	17.917	17.201	125.206	117.911	112.033
Accumulated Depreciation	5.680	4.572	88.166	84.600	79.047
Net Plant, Property, and Equipment	12.237	12.629	37.040	33.311	32.986
Investments at Equity	0.000	0.000	5.343	5.534	4.949
Other Investments	10.229	0.000	28.285	34.638	32.144
Intangibles	25.426	26.662	28.280	10.737	0.000
Other Assets	2.910	28.655	3.421	4.450	2.729
TOTAL ASSETS	90.002	95.771	143.953	135.589	136.929
LIABILITIES					
Long-Term Debt Due in One Year	1.474	0.300	0.082	0.000	0.000
Notes Payable	0.000	0.000	3.000	0.000	0.000
Accounts Payable	1.281	1.454	8.421	8.358	9.611
Taxes Payable	0.000	0.064	1.215	0.692	0.932
Other Current Liabilities	1.468	3.746	10.964	9.011	8.424
Total Current Liabilities	4.223	5.564	23.682	18.061	18.967
Long-Term Debt	4.499	5.973	4.679	0.000	0.000
Deferred Taxes	0.000	0.381	8.251	9.295	8.789
Minority Interest	0.000	0.000	2.479	2.227	1.690
Other Liabilities	11.947	0.646	15.825	15.886	15.928
EQUITY					
Common Stock	0.858	0.858	0.858	0.858	0.858
Capital Surplus	5.392	5.847	5.856	5.842	5.834
Retained Earnings	64.576	79.903	85.769	86.895	88.368
Less: Treasury Stock	1.493	3.401	3.446	3.475	3.505
Common Equity	69.333	83.207	89.037	90.120	91.555
TOTAL EQUITY	69.333	83.207	89.037	90.120	91.555
TOTAL LIABILITIES AND EQUITY	90.002	95.771	143.953	135.589	136.929
COMMON SHARES OUTSTANDING	1.674	1.620	1.619	1.618	1.617

3. Construct common form income statements from the income statement of the following firms, determine their operating strategies, and discuss the implications.

a. Coors

Annual Income Statement ($ Million, except per Share)	Dec00	Dec99	Dec98	Dec97	Dec96
Sales	2,414.415	2,056.646	1,899.533	1,822.151	1,732.233
Cost of Goods Sold	1,396.546	1,092.195	1,043.072	1,003.612	996.745
Gross Profit	1,017.869	964.451	856.461	818.539	735.488
Selling, General, and Administrative Expense	722.745	692.993	617.432	585.491	527.007
Operating Income before Depreciation	295.124	271.458	239.029	233.048	208.481
Depreciation, Depletion, and Amortization	129.283	123.770	115.815	117.166	121.121
Operating Profit	165.841	147.688	123.214	115.882	87.360
Interest Expense	6.414	8.478	12.532	15.460	17.057
Non-Operating Income/Expense	25.313	17.162	19.813	14.954	11.013
Special Items	(15.215)	(5.705)	(19.395)	31.517	(6.341)
Pretax Income	169.525	150.667	111.100	146.893	74.975
Total Income Taxes	59.908	58.383	43.316	64.633	31.550
Income before Extraordinary Items and Discontinued Operations	109.617	92.284	67.784	82.260	43.425
Available for Common	109.617	92.284	67.784	82.260	43.425
Adjusted Available for Common	109.617	92.284	67.784	82.260	43.425
Adjusted Net Income	109.617	92.284	67.784	82.260	43.425

b. Genesee

Annual Income Statement *($ Millions, except per Share*	*Apr01*	*Apr00*	*Apr99*	*Apr98*	*Apr97*
Sales	46.533	45.548	150.007	154.093	154.543
Cost of Goods Sold	35.853	36.568	106.998	112.150	111.796
Gross Profit	10.680	8.980	43.009	41.943	42.747
Selling, General, and Administrative Expense	8.182	7.801	36.070	36.346	34.979
Operating Income before Depreciation	2.498	1.179	6.939	5.597	7.768
Depreciation, Depletion, and Amortization	3.009	2.853	6.591	6.285	5.172
Operating Profit	(0.511)	(1.674)	0.348	(0.688)	2.596
Interest Expense	0.422	0.351	0.873	0.000	0.000
Non-Operating Income/Expense	1.429	0.734	6.320	3.801	3.279
Special Items	(1.600)	0.000	0.000	0.000	0.000
Pretax Income	(1.104)	(1.291)	5.795	3.113	5.875
Total Income Taxes	(0.040)	(0.150)	2.095	0.974	1.831
Minority Interest	0.000	0.000	1.237	0.804	0.698
Income before Extraordinary Items and Discontinued Operations	(1.064)	(1.141)	2.463	1.335	3.346
Available for Common	(1.064)	(1.141)	2.463	1.335	3.346
Savings Due to Common Stock Equivalents	0.000	0.000	0.000	0.000	0.000
Adjusted Available for Common	(1.064)	(1.141)	2.463	1.335	3.346
Discontinued Operations	(1.350)	(2.259)	0.000	0.000	0.000
Adjusted Net Income	(2.414)	(3.400)	2.463	1.335	3.346

c. Red Hook

Annual Income Statement *($ Millions, except per Share)*	*Dec00*	*Dec99*	*Dec98*	*Dec97*	*Dec96*
Sales	34.412	32.194	32.641	34.286	35.678
Cost of Goods Sold	21.340	19.342	20.574	22.564	21.538
Gross Profit	13.072	12.852	12.067	11.722	14.140
Selling, General, and Administrative Expense	11.747	11.290	9.086	9.981	7.853
Operating Income before Depreciation	1.325	1.562	2.981	1.741	6.287
Depreciation, Depletion, and Amortization	3.240	3.271	3.343	3.399	2.043
Operating Profit	(1.915)	(1.709)	(0.362)	(1.658)	4.244
Interest Expense	0.594	0.534	0.679	0.648	0.291
Non-Operating Income/Expense	0.443	(0.048)	0.127	0.363	0.906
Special Items	1.010	0.000	(5.173)	0.000	0.000
Pretax Income	(1.056)	(2.291)	(6.087)	(1.943)	4.859
Total Income Taxes	(0.328)	(0.768)	(2.076)	(0.544)	1.773
Income before Extraordinary Items and Discontinued Operations	(0.728)	(1.523)	(4.011)	(1.399)	3.086
Preferred Dividends	0.000	0.000	0.000	0.000	0.044
Available for Common	(0.728)	(1.523)	(4.011)	(1.399)	3.042
Savings Due to Common Stock Equivalents	0.000	0.000	0.000	0.000	0.044
Adjusted Available for Common	(0.728)	(1.523)	(4.011)	(1.399)	3.086
Adjusted Net Income	(0.728)	(1.523)	(4.011)	(1.399)	3.086

4. For the firms listed, determine the stage of growth based on an analysis of their financial statements.

   a. Remec, Inc.

Annual Balance Sheet ($ Millions)	Jan01	Jan00	Jan99	Jan98	Jan97
ASSETS					
Cash and Equivalents	138.526	34.836	83.011	41.937	63.173
Net Receivables	49.678	33.112	27.295	25.495	15.973
Inventories	58.866	42.147	38.312	30.381	19.332
Prepaid Expenses	0.000	0.000	0.000	0.000	0.000
Other Current Assets	19.152	10.086	8.022	6.831	3.616
Total Current Assets	266.222	120.181	156.640	104.644	102.094
Gross Plant, Property, and Equipment	144.849	113.621	86.421	64.188	45.961
Accumulated Depreciation	62.008	53.331	41.714	32.199	27.418
Net Plant, Property, and Equipment	82.841	60.290	44.707	31.989	18.543
Other Assets	41.161	43.458	17.224	17.232	4.803
TOTAL ASSETS	390.224	223.929	218.571	153.865	125.440
LIABILITIES					
Long-Term Debt Due in One Year	0.000	0.225	0.000	0.000	0.482
Notes Payable	0.000	0.000	0.075	0.000	1.891
Accounts Payable	19.948	8.320	8.156	8.532	5.974
Taxes Payable	1.271	1.250	0.000	2.546	2.249
Accrued Expenses	0.000	0.000	14.602	9.070	7.386
Other Current Liabilities	19.599	14.776	0.000	0.000	0.000
Total Current Liabilities	40.818	24.571	22.833	20.148	17.982
Long-Term Debt	0.000	5.049	0.000	0.000	2.462
Deferred Taxes	6.457	6.417	4.131	5.118	1.179
Investment Tax Credit	0.000	0.000	0.000	0.000	0.000
Minority Interest	1.462	0.000	0.000	0.000	0.000
Other Liabilities	0.000	0.000	0.000	0.104	0.262
EQUITY					
Common Stock	0.447	0.254	0.249	0.212	0.137
Capital Surplus	317.203	170.133	165.633	95.303	85.856
Retained Earnings	23.837	17.505	25.725	32.980	17.562
Common Equity	341.487	187.892	191.607	128.495	103.555
TOTAL EQUITY	341.487	187.892	191.607	128.495	103.555
TOTAL LIABILITIES AND EQUITY	390.224	223.929	218.571	153.865	125.440
COMMON SHARES OUTSTANDING	44.669	38.145	37.320	31.775	30.802

Annual Income Statement ($ Millions, except per Share)	Jan01	Jan00	Jan99	Jan98	Jan97
Sales	273.499	189.189	179.215	156.057	118.554
Cost of Goods Sold	191.396	132.094	127.512	102.672	82.010
Gross Profit	82.103	57.095	51.703	53.385	36.544
Selling, General, and Administrative Expense	64.574	52.183	47.739	28.781	23.531
Operating Income before Depreciation	17.529	4.912	3.964	24.604	13.013
Depreciation, Depletion, and Amortization	12.416	11.486	9.930	5.381	3.648
Operating Profit	5.113	(6.574)	(5.966)	19.223	9.365
Interest Expense	0.000	0.000	0.000	0.000	0.000
Non-Operating Income/Expense	11.509	2.601	3.008	2.280	0.048
Special Items	(2.750)	(3.130)	0.000	1.733	(0.424)
Pretax Income	13.872	(7.103)	(2.958)	23.236	8.989
Total Income Taxes	2.917	(0.428)	1.873	8.501	4.017
Minority Interest	0.076	0.000	0.000	0.000	0.000
Income before Extraordinary Items and Discontinued Operations	10.879	(6.675)	(4.831)	14.735	4.972
Preferred Dividends	0.000	0.000	0.000	0.000	0.000
Available for Common	10.879	(6.675)	(4.831)	14.735	4.972
Savings Due to Common Stock Equivalents	0.000	0.000	0.000	0.000	0.000
Adjusted Available for Common	10.879	(6.675)	(4.831)	14.735	4.972
Extraordinary Items	0.000	0.000	0.000	0.000	0.000
Discontinued Operations	0.000	0.000	0.000	0.000	0.000
Adjusted Net Income	10.879	(6.675)	(4.831)	14.735	4.972

Annual Statement of Cash Flows *($ Millions)*	*Jan01*	*Jan00*	*Jan99*	*Jan98*	*Jan97*
INDIRECT OPERATING ACTIVITIES					
Income before Extraordinary Items	10.879	(6.675)	(4.831)	14.735	4.972
Depreciation and Amortization	16.207	13.378	9.930	5.381	3.648
Extraordinary Items and Discontinued					
Operations	0.000	0.000	0.000	0.000	0.000
Deferred Taxes	(7.106)	(1.925)	1.310	(2.408)	(0.767)
Sale of Property, Plant, and Equipment					
and Sale of Investments—Loss (Gain)	0.000	0.000	0.000	(2.833)	0.000
Funds from Operations—Other	9.590	0.000	0.139	0.000	0.000
Receivables—Decrease (Increase)	(16.644)	(6.678)	7.079	(6.525)	(4.863)
Inventory—Decrease (Increase)	(16.806)	(2.553)	(1.584)	(9.304)	(2.539)
Other Assets and Liabilities—Net Change	14.140	4.490	(5.780)	1.741	0.378
Operating Activities—Net Cash Flow	10.260	0.037	6.263	0.787	0.829
INVESTING ACTIVITIES					
Investments—Increase	0.000	0.000	0.000	0.000	0.000
Sale of Investments	0.000	0.000	0.000	0.000	0.000
Short-Term Investments—Change	0.000	0.000	0.000	0.000	1.483
Capital Expenditures	34.547	23.199	18.279	17.351	7.363
Sale of Property, Plant, and Equipment	0.000	0.000	0.000	0.000	0.000
Acquisitions	0.000	5.825	0.000	5.066	4.012
Investing Activities—Other	(4.739)	(26.840)	(1.589)	5.120	(0.146)
Investing Activities—Net Cash Flow	(39.286)	(55.864)	(19.868)	(17.297)	(10.038)
FINANCING ACTIVITIES					
Sale of Common and Preferred Stock	138.195	3.349	52.676	2.898	71.261
Purchase of Common and Preferred Stock	0.000	0.000	2.851	0.000	0.000
Cash Dividends	0.000	0.000	0.000	0.000	0.000
Long-Term Debt—Issuance	0.000	6.026	0.000	12.213	1.100
Long-Term Debt—Reduction	5.277	1.466	0.000	19.510	3.413
Current Debt—Changes	0.000	0.000	(1.391)	0.000	0.000
Financing Activities—Other	0.000	0.000	0.000	0.000	1.109
Financing Activities—Net Cash Flow	132.918	7.909	48.434	(4.399)	70.057
Exchange Rate Effect	(0.202)	0.005	0.217	0.000	0.000
Cash and Equivalents—Change	103.690	(47.913)	35.046	(20.909)	60.848
DIRECT OPERATING ACTIVITIES					
Interest Paid—Net	0.074	0.208	0.098	0.321	0.414
Income Taxes Paid	0.238	0.808	4.661	10.162	3.091

b. Hormel Foods Corp.

Annual Balance Sheet ($ Millions)	Oct00	Oct99	Oct98	Oct97	Oct96
ASSETS					
Cash and Equivalents	106.610	248.562	238.032	152.386	203.115
Net Receivables	307.732	266.059	222.919	233.966	230.869
Inventories	281.404	270.239	239.548	265.346	271.097
Prepaid Expenses	6.342	5.757	7.972	7.450	6.563
Other Current Assets	9.021	9.526	8.894	12.204	11.615
Total Current Assets	711.109	800.143	717.365	671.352	723.259
Gross Plant, Property, and Equipment	1,081.612	1,002.186	938.581	919.929	828.614
Accumulated Depreciation	540.063	496.562	451.674	431.191	407.128
Net Plant, Property, and Equipment	541.549	505.624	486.907	488.738	421.486
Other Investments	151.383	142.879	111.364	113.372	0.000
Intangibles	92.632	98.544	105.244	131.710	124.193
Other Assets	145.267	138.395	135.012	123.363	167.200
TOTAL ASSETS	1,641.940	1,685.585	1,555.892	1,528.535	1,436.138
LIABILITIES					
Long-Term Debt Due in One Year	38.439	41.214	6.117	4.595	2.548
Accounts Payable	154.893	162.585	119.836	120.385	121.004
Taxes Payable	2.609	12.186	1.172	4.712	9.804
Accrued Expenses	134.489	157.520	128.752	118.906	121.442
Other Current Liabilities	12.195	11.902	11.774	11.980	11.611
Total Current Liabilities	342.625	385.407	267.651	260.578	266.409
Long-Term Debt	145.928	184.723	204.874	198.232	127.003
Other Liabilities	279.510	274.313	270.052	267.523	257.175
EQUITY					
Common Stock	8.120	8.364	8.628	8.881	9.087
Capital Surplus	0.000	0.000	0.000	0.000	32.214
Retained Earnings	865.757	832.778	808.246	793.321	744.785
Less: Treasury Stock	0.000	0.000	3.559	0.000	0.535
Common Equity	873.877	841.142	813.315	802.202	785.551
TOTAL EQUITY	873.877	841.142	813.315	802.202	785.551
TOTAL LIABILITIES AND EQUITY	1,641.940	1,685.585	1,555.892	1,528.535	1,436.138
COMMON SHARES OUTSTANDING	138.569	142.724	146.992	151.554	155.020

Annual Income Statement ($ Millions, except per Share)	Oct00	Oct99	Oct98	Oct97	Oct96
Sales	3,675.132	3,357.757	3,261.045	3,256.551	3,098.685
Cost of Goods Sold	2,608.988	2,315.069	2,340.060	2,444.737	2,355.573
Gross Profit	1,066.144	1,042.688	920.985	811.814	743.112
Selling, General, and Administrative Expense	737.651	737.125	677.207	590.719	578.767
Operating Income before Depreciation	328.493	305.563	243.778	221.095	164.345
Depreciation, Depletion, and Amortization	65.886	64.656	60.273	52.925	42.699
Operating Profit	262.607	240.907	183.505	168.170	121.646
Interest Expense	14.906	13.746	13.692	15.043	1.619
Non-Operating Income/Expense	16.680	24.312	19.144	12.558	14.106
Special Items	0.000	0.000	28.379	5.176	(8.659)
Pretax Income	264.381	251.473	217.336	170.861	125.474
Total Income Taxes	94.164	88.035	78.045	61.369	46.066
Income before Extraordinary Items and Discontinued Operations	170.217	163.438	139.291	109.492	79.408
Available for Common	170.217	163.438	139.291	109.492	79.408
Adjusted Net Income	170.217	163.438	139.291	109.492	79.408

Annual Statement of Cash Flows ($ Millions)	Oct00	Oct99	Oct98	Oct97	Oct96
INDIRECT OPERATING ACTIVITIES					
Income before Extraordinary Items	170.217	163.438	139.291	109.492	79.408
Depreciation and Amortization	65.886	64.656	60.273	52.925	42.699
Deferred Taxes	7.160	1.968	4.516	(0.444)	(2.347)
Equity in Net Loss (Earnings)	3.083	(4.830)	(4.323)	(3.402)	0.000
Sale of Property, Plant, and Equipment and Sale of Investments—Loss (Gain)	0.360	1.293	(15.346)	@CF	@CF
Funds from Operations—Other	0.000	0.000	0.000	0.050	(8.394)
Receivables—Decrease (Increase)	(41.673)	(43.140)	11.047	(3.097)	2.773
Inventory—Decrease (Increase)	0.000	0.000	0.000	0.000	0.000
Accounts Payable and Accrued Liabilities—Increase (Decrease)	(38.420)	86.792	8.286	2.101	52.040
Income Taxes—Accrued— Increase (Decrease)	0.000	0.000	0.000	0.000	0.000
Other Assets and Liabilities—Net Change	(11.750)	(28.476)	25.276	4.864	(56.771)
Operating Activities—Net Cash Flow	154.863	241.701	229.020	162.489	109.408
INVESTING ACTIVITIES					
Sale of Investments	0.000	0.000	@CF	0.000	0.000
Short-Term Investments—Change	54.288	(26.154)	(28.565)	9.109	(1.526)
Capital Expenditures	100.125	79.121	75.774	116.381	122.942
Sale of Property, Plant, and Equipment	3.866	1.155	39.792	4.163	5.410
Acquisitions	0.000	0.000	0.000	0.140	12.845
Investing Activities—Other	(36.044)	(42.177)	5.722	(81.805)	(18.418)
Investing Activities—Net Cash Flow	(78.015)	(146.297)	(58.825)	(185.054)	(150.321)
FINANCING ACTIVITIES					
Purchase of Common and Preferred Stock	75.330	87.636	80.076	45.457	23.966
Cash Dividends	48.735	47.858	47.678	47.178	45.613
Long-Term Debt—Issuance	4.439	26.100	17.589	77.625	110.553
Long-Term Deb— Reduction	43.183	4.778	4.312	4.349	3.393
Current Debt—Changes	0.000	0.000	0.000	0.000	0.000
Financing Activities—Other	(1.703)	3.144	1.363	0.304	2.266
Financing Activities—Net Cash Flow	(164.512)	(111.028)	(113.114)	(19.055)	39.847
Exchange Rate Effect	0.000	0.000	0.000	0.000	0.000
Cash and Equivalents—Change	(87.664)	(15.624)	57.081	(41.620)	(1.066)
DIRECT OPERATING ACTIVITIES					
Interest Paid—Net	14.800	14.800	13.600	14.908	1.629
Income Taxes Paid	98.100	76.400	76.500	66.500	38.263

c. Diametrics Medical, Inc.

Annual Balance Sheet ($ Millions)	Dec00	Dec99	Dec98	Dec97	Dec96
ASSETS					
Cash and Equivalents	8.714	14.126	6.409	11.761	5.855
Net Receivables	6.682	6.791	5.420	3.768	2.589
Inventories	4.280	4.116	4.768	3.588	4.464
Prepaid Expenses	0.000	0.000	0.000	0.000	0.000
Other Current Assets	0.397	0.285	0.454	0.311	0.544
Total Current Assets	20.073	25.318	17.051	19.428	13.452
Gross Plant, Property, and Equipment	22.475	19.455	20.077	18.060	16.296
Accumulated Depreciation	15.138	13.681	13.155	10.674	8.008
Net Plant, Property, and Equipment	7.337	5.774	6.922	7.386	8.288
Intangibles	0.000	0.148	0.223	1.820	2.260
Other Assets	0.401	0.732	1.150	0.028	0.059
TOTAL ASSETS	27.811	31.972	25.346	28.662	24.059
LIABILITIES					
Long-Term Debt Due in One Year	0.426	0.350	0.417	0.970	1.250
Notes Payable	0.000	0.000	0.829	0.000	0.032
Accounts Payable	2.400	2.439	2.535	2.262	1.613
Accrued Expenses	1.914	2.415	1.855	3.687	3.848
Other Current Liabilities	1.000	5.104	0.000	0.000	0.060
Total Current Liabilities	5.740	10.308	5.636	6.919	6.803
Long-Term Debt	7.472	7.814	8.163	8.538	8.463
Other Liabilities	0.414	0.009	0.181	0.062	0.119
EQUITY					
Common Stock	0.267	0.258	0.234	0.209	0.152
Capital Surplus	147.292	143.463	130.478	113.970	88.452
Retained Earnings	(133.374)	(129.880)	(119.346)	(101.036)	(79.930)
Common Equity	14.185	13.841	11.366	13.143	8.674
TOTAL EQUITY	14.185	13.841	11.366	13.143	8.674
TOTAL LIABILITIES AND EQUITY	27.811	31.972	25.346	28.662	24.059
COMMON SHARES OUTSTANDING	26.713	25.778	20.890	20.890	15.209

Annual Income Statement ($ Millions, except per Share)	Dec00	Dec99	Dec98	Dec97	Dec96
Sales	25.258	18.687	12.156	10.434	3.797
Cost of Goods Sold	15.581	13.556	8.188	7.503	6.477
Gross Profit	9.677	5.131	3.968	2.931	(2.680)
Selling, General, and Administrative Expense	10.263	12.951	17.737	18.814	16.653
Operating Income before Depreciation	(0.586)	(7.820)	(13.769)	(15.883)	(19.333)
Depreciation, Depletion, and Amortization	2.157	2.225	3.147	4.163	3.114
Operating Profit	(2.743)	(10.045)	(16.916)	(20.046)	(22.447)
Interest Expense	0.587	0.630	0.807	1.018	0.607
Non-Operating Income/Expense	0.682	0.431	0.335	0.491	0.814
Special Items	0.000	0.000	0.000	(0.464)	(1.335)
Pretax Income	(2.648)	(10.244)	(17.388)	(21.037)	(23.575)
Total Income Taxes	0.000	0.000	0.000	0.000	0.000
Adjusted Net Income	(2.648)	(10.244)	(17.388)	(21.037)	(23.575)

Annual Statement of Cash Flows ($ Millions)	Dec00	Dec99	Dec98	Dec97	Dec96
INDIRECT OPERATING ACTIVITIES					
Income before Extraordinary Items	(2.648)	(10.244)	(17.388)	(21.037)	(23.575)
Depreciation and Amortization	2.157	2.225	3.147	4.163	3.114
Sale of Property, Plant, and Equipment and Sale of Investments—Loss (Gain)	0.000	0.000	0.001	(0.081)	(0.002)
Funds from Operation—Other	0.000	0.013	(0.652)	0.029	0.465
Receivables—Decrease (Increase)	0.109	(1.371)	(1.652)	(1.179)	(0.581)
Inventory—Decrease (Increase)	(0.164)	0.651	(1.326)	0.876	(0.632)
Accounts Payable and Accrued Liabilities—Increase (Decrease)	(0.647)	0.405	(1.506)	0.418	0.348
Income Taxes—Accrued—Increase (Decrease)	0.000	0.000	0.000	0.000	0.000
Other Assets and Liabilities—Net Change	(4.217)	5.275	(0.044)	0.233	0.523
Operating Activities—Net Cash Flow	(5.410)	(3.046)	(19.420)	(16.578)	(20.340)
INVESTING ACTIVITIES					
Short-Term Investments—Change	5.058	(8.363)	5.426	(4.999)	22.387
Capital Expenditures	3.438	1.689	2.253	2.958	1.597
Sale of Property, Plant, and Equipment	0.000	0.945	0.000	0.237	0.102
Acquisitions	0.000	0.000	0.000	0.000	1.068
Investing Activities—Other	0.004	0.026	0.012	(0.037)	(0.037)
Investing Activities—Net Cash Flow	1.624	(9.081)	3.185	(7.757)	19.787
FINANCING ACTIVITIES					
Sale of Common and Preferred Stock	3.837	12.996	16.519	25.547	0.966
Long-Term Debt—Issuance	0.116	0.000	1.819	1.058	0.500
Long-Term Debt—Reduction	0.371	1.245	1.918	1.295	1.079
Current Debt—Changes	0.000	0.000	0.000	0.000	(0.108)
Financing Activities—Net Cash Flow	3.582	11.751	16.420	25.310	0.279
Exchange Rate Effect	(0.150)	(0.270)	(0.111)	(0.068)	0.024
Cash and Equivalents—Change	(0.354)	(0.646)	0.074	0.907	(0.250)
DIRECT OPERATING ACTIVITIES					
Interest Paid—Net	0.587	0.630	1.544	0.378	0.510

5. Perform a Du Pont analysis for the firms in the table that follows:

Du Pont Analysis of Food Processing Industry's 2000 Results				
Company Name	Sales-Net	Assets-Total	Net Income (Loss)	Stockholders' Equity
Dean Foods Company	4,065.636	2,003.542	106.118	657.685
Dreyer's Grand Ice Cream Inc.	1,194.356	468.451	25.378	200.912
Earthgrains Company	2,039.300	2,339.500	54.500	654.900
Flowers Foods Inc.	1,619.980	1,562.646	5.045	502.460
Interstate Bakeries Corp.	3,522.929	1,651.925	89.388	591.677
International Multifoods Corp.	2,384.715	736.207	5.135	255.124
Pro-Fac Cooperative Inc.	1,268.542	1,187.266	16.164	159.843
Quaker Oats Company	5,041.000	2,418.800	360.600	376.300
Suiza Foods Corp.	5,756.303	3,780.478	118.719	598.832
Tofutti Brands Inc.	13.343	4.813	0.956	3.953
Wrigley (WM) Jr. Company	2,145.706	1,574.740	328.942	1,132.897

6. Using the information in the financial statements of American Greetings, calculate the following ratios:

Annual Ratio Report (Ratio, except as Noted)	Feb01	Feb00	Feb99	Feb98	Feb97	Feb96
LIQUIDITY						
Current Ratio						
Quick Ratio						
Working Capital per Share						
ACTIVITY						
Inventory Turnover						
Receivables Turnover						
Total Asset Turnover						
PERFORMANCE						
Sales/Net Property, Plant, and Equipment						
Sales/Stockholder Equity						
PROFITABILITY						
Operating Margin before Depreciation (%)						
Operating Margin after Depreciation (%)						
Pretax Profit Margin (%)						
Net Profit Margin (%)						
Return on Assets (%)						
Return on Equity (%)						
Return on Investment (%)						
Return on Average Assets (%)						
Return on Average Equity (%)						
LEVERAGE						
Interest Coverage before Tax						
Interest Coverage after Tax						
Long-Term Debt/Common Equity (%)						
Long-Term Debt/Shareholder Equity(%)						
Total Debt/Total Assets (%)						
Total Assets/Common Equity						
Dividend Payout (%)						

Annual Balance Sheet *($ Millions)*	*Feb01*	*Feb00*	*Feb99*	*Feb98*	*Feb97*
ASSETS					
Cash and Equivalents	51.691	61.010	144.555	47.623	35.050
Net Receivables	387.534	430.825	390.740	373.594	375.324
Inventories	365.221	249.433	251.289	271.205	303.611
Other Current Assets	401.290	359.416	359.234	330.823	290.906
Total Current Assets	1,205.736	1,100.684	1,145.818	1,023.245	1,004.891
Gross Plant, Property, and Equipment	1,086.094	1,019.121	958.623	938.743	920.194
Accumulated Depreciation	608.906	571.706	523.817	491.111	457.407
Net Plant, Property, and Equipment	477.188	447.415	434.806	447.632	462.787
Intangibles	229.802	149.437	135.516	0.000	0.000
Deferred Charges	717.400	679.214	595.136	481.236	464.599
Other Assets	81.948	141.233	108.052	193.779	202.843
TOTAL ASSETS	2,712.074	2,517.983	2,419.328	2,145.892	2,135.120
LIABILITIES					
Long-Term Debt Due in One Year	0.664	2.279	2.218	47.200	0.436
Notes Payable	378.240	107.415	15.559	152.440	132.735
Accounts Payable	304.063	213.180	175.366	145.554	157.628
Taxes Payable	192.936	13.090	27.165	22.536	5.475
Other Current Liabilities	235.378	246.524	197.366	149.486	146.469
Total Current Liabilities	1,111.281	582.488	417.674	517.216	442.743
Long-Term Debt	380.124	442.102	463.246	148.800	219.639
Deferred Taxes	27.292	44.997	49.752	42.722	43.244
Other Liabilities	146.187	195.985	142.045	91.937	67.839
EQUITY					
Common Stock	63.489	64.520	69.093	71.182	74.982
Capital Surplus	286.054	304.946	304.086	290.820	272.262
Retained Earnings	1,144.774	1,328.703	1,293.924	1,183.595	1,049.261
Less: Treasury Stock	447.127	445.758	320.492	200.380	34.850
Common Equity	1,047.190	1,252.411	1,346.611	1,345.217	1,361.655
TOTAL EQUITY	1,047.190	1,252.411	1,346.611	1,345.217	1,361.655
TOTAL LIABILITIES AND EQUITY	2,712.074	2,517.983	2,419.328	2,145.892	2,135.120
COMMON SHARES OUTSTANDING	63.489	64.520	69.093	71.183	74.982

Annual Income Statement ($ Millions, except per Share)	Feb01	Feb00	Feb99	Feb98	Feb97
Sales	2,518.814	2,175.236	2,205.706	2,198.765	2,161.089
Cost of Goods Sold	901.214	737.323	690.031	724.762	740.558
Gross Profit	1,617.600	1,437.913	1,515.675	1,474.003	1,420.531
Selling, General, and Administrative Expense	1,348.745	1,148.467	1,122.506	1,128.122	1,082.095
Operating Income before Depreciation	268.855	289.446	393.169	345.881	338.436
Depreciation, Depletion, and Amortization	98.057	64.342	67.049	65.926	64.566
Operating Profit	170.798	225.104	326.120	279.955	273.870
Interest Expense	55.387	34.255	29.326	22.992	30.749
Non-Operating Income/Expense	7.376	(3.670)	(1.272)	13.349	11.209
Special Items	(24.154)	(46.555)	(13.925)	22.125	0.000
Pretax Income	98.633	140.624	281.597	292.437	254.330
Total Income Taxes	191.306	50.625	101.375	102.353	87.235
Income before Extraordinary Items and Discontinued Operations	(92.673)	89.999	180.222	190.084	167.095
Extraordinary Items	(21.141)	0.000	0.000	0.000	0.000
Adjusted Net Income	(113.814)	89.999	180.222	190.084	167.095

Annual Statement of Cash Flows ($ Millions)	Feb01	Feb00	Feb99	Feb98	Feb97
INDIRECT OPERATING ACTIVITIES					
Income before Extraordinary Items	(92.673)	89.999	180.222	190.084	167.095
Depreciation and Amortization	98.057	64.342	67.049	65.926	64.566
Extraordinary Items and Discontinued					
Operations	0.000	0.000	0.000	0.000	0.000
Deferred Taxes	61.227	54.248	(8.940)	(20.186)	0.294
Funds from Operations—Other	36.501	42.548	10.226	5.018	5.100
Receivables—Decrease (Increase)	29.201	(35.883)	(10.450)	(20.567)	(25.389)
Inventory—Decrease (Increase)	(46.587)	11.655	17.809	5.915	32.371
Other Assets and Liabilities—Net Change	24.074	(58.390)	(44.648)	(8.873)	(90.134)
Operating Activities—Net Cash Flow	109.800	168.519	211.268	195.192	153.903
INVESTING ACTIVITIES					
Capital Expenditures	74.382	50.753	60.950	67.898	92.895
Sale of Property, Plant, and Equipment	22.294	1.490	2.522	2.148	2.579
Acquisitions	179.993	65.947	52.957	0.000	0.000
Investing Activities—Other	34.125	(22.437)	26.453	77.699	(14.737)
Investing Activities—Net Cash Flow	(197.956)	(137.647)	(84.932)	11.949	(105.053)
FINANCING ACTIVITIES					
Sale of Common and Preferred Stock	0.000	1.171	18.981	16.915	6.997
Purchase of Common and Preferred Stock	45.530	130.151	131.745	170.015	1.863
Cash Dividends	52.743	51.213	52.410	51.959	50.152
Long-Term Debt—Issuance	0.000	1.076	317.096	9.430	8.451
Long-Term Debt—Reduction	80.431	16.397	22.669	6.988	12.232
Current Debt—Changes	257.541	81.097	(158.657)	8.049	4.869
Financing Activities—Other	0.000	0.000	0.000	0.000	0.000
Financing Activities—Net Cash Flow	78.837	(114.417)	(29.404)	(194.568)	(43.930)
Exchange Rate Effect	0.000	0.000	0.000	0.000	0.000
Cash and Equivalents—Change	(9.319)	(83.545)	96.932	12.573	4.920
DIRECT OPERATING ACTIVITIES					
Interest Paid—Net	54.637	34.051	27.831	22.735	29.914
Income Taxes Paid	(18.174)	19.821	102.363	101.261	99.391

7. Using the information in the financial statements of Solectron Corp, calculate the following ratios:

Annual Ratio Report (Ratio, except as Noted)	Aug01	Aug00	Aug99	Aug98	Aug97	Aug96
LIQUIDITY						
Current Ratio						
Quick Ratio						
Working Capital per Share						
ACTIVITY						
Inventory Turnover						
Receivables Turnover						
Total Asset Turnover						
PERFORMANCE						
Sales/Net Property, Plant, and Equipment						
Sales/Stockholder Equity						
PROFITABILITY						
Operating Margin before Depreciation (%)						
Operating Margin after Depreciation (%)						
Pretax Profit Margin (%)						
Net Profit Margin (%)						
Return on Assets (%)						
Return on Equity (%)						
Return on Investment (%)						
Return on Average Assets (%)						
Return on Average Equity (%)						
LEVERAGE						
Interest Coverage before Tax						
Interest Coverage after Tax						
Long-Term Debt/Common Equity (%)						
Long-Term Debt/Shareholder Equity(%)						
Total Debt/Total Assets (%)						
Total Assets/Common Equity						
Dividend Payout (%)						

Annual Balance Sheet ($ Millions)	Aug01	Aug00	Aug99	Aug98	Aug97
ASSETS					
Cash and Equivalents	2,790.100	2,434.100	1,688.400	308.804	482.902
Net Receivables	2,443.600	2,146.300	1,118.300	670.194	418.682
Inventories	3,209.900	3,787.300	1,080.100	788.519	494.622
Other Current Assets	260.500	260.500	107.300	120.041	79.426
Total Current Assets	8,704.100	8,628.200	3,994.100	1,887.558	1,475.632
Gross Plant, Property, and 　Equipment	2,511.800	1,849.800	1,186.900	859.831	648.777
Accumulated Depreciation	1,207.100	769.400	533.300	411.792	322.416
Net Plant, Property, and Equipment	1,304.700	1,080.400	653.600	448.039	326.361
Other Assets	2,921.600	667.000	187.000	74.971	50.426
TOTAL ASSETS	12,930.400	10,375.600	4,834.700	2,410.568	1,852.419
LIABILITIES					
Long-Term Debt Due in One Year	0.000	0.000	0.000	2.821	1.464
Notes Payable	306.200	69.200	21.400	0.000	0.000
Accounts Payable	1,786.100	2,694.100	902.600	666.557	415.896
Accrued Expenses	530.200	442.300	129.300	106.959	81.005
Other Current Liabilities	66.800	11.200	59.900	64.497	45.577
Total Current Liabilities	2,689.300	3,216.800	1,113.200	840.834	543.942
Long-Term Debt	5,027.500	3,319.500	922.600	385.519	385.850
Other Liabilities	62.900	37.200	5.800	2.889	3.558
EQUITY					
Common Stock	0.700	0.600	0.300	0.117	0.115
Capital Surplus	3,877.600	2,259.100	1,910.100	510.757	451.093
Retained Earnings	1,272.400	1,542.400	882.700	670.452	467.861
Common Equity	5,150.700	3,802.100	2,793.100	1,181.326	919.069
TOTAL EQUITY	5,150.700	3,802.100	2,793.100	1,181.326	919.069
TOTAL LIABILITIES AND EQUITY	12,930.400	10,375.600	4,834.700	2,410.568	1,852.419
COMMON SHARES OUTSTANDING	658.200	605.000	542.800	470.668	458.184

Annual Income Statement
($ Millions, except per Share)

	Aug01	Aug00	Aug99	Aug98	Aug97
Sales	18,692.301	14,137.500	8,391.400	5,288.294	3,694.385
Cost of Goods Sold	16,810.000	12,610.800	7,431.400	4,625.788	3,161.516
Gross Profit	1,882.301	1,526.700	960.000	662.506	532.869
Selling, General, and Administrative Expense	897.800	533.200	337.900	239.317	187.857
Operating Income before Depreciation	984.500	993.500	622.100	423.189	345.012
Depreciation, Depletion, and Amortization	536.100	251.400	183.200	124.200	104.590
Operating Profit	448.400	742.100	438.900	298.989	240.422
Interest Expense	176.000	71.600	39.700	26.459	26.551
Non-Operating Income/Expense	116.900	106.900	33.100	26.453	28.536
Special Items	(547.000)	(37.900)	0.000	0.000	(4.000)
Pretax Income	(157.700)	739.500	432.300	298.983	238.407
Total Income Taxes	(34.200)	238.800	138.400	100.159	80.348
Net Income	(123.500)	497.200	293.900	198.824	158.059

Annual Statement of Cash Flows
($ Millions)

	Aug01	Aug00	Aug99	Aug98	Aug97
INDIRECT OPERATING ACTIVITIES					
Income before Extraordinary Items	(123.500)	500.700	293.900	198.824	158.059
Depreciation and Amortization	0.000	251.400	183.200	124.200	104.590
Sale of Property, Plant, and Equipment and Sale of Investments—Loss (Gain)	(10.000)	(8.700)	(4.900)	(2.277)	0.000
Funds from Operations—Other	1,063.700	121.700	53.900	8.039	14.316
Receivables—Decrease (Increase)	52.400	(934.100)	(458.300)	(250.575)	(66.293)
Inventory—Decrease (Increase)	1,024.100	(2,096.000)	(288.200)	(164.058)	(115.560)
Other Assets and Liabilities— Net Change	(1,379.100)	1,822.300	258.400	235.632	117.464
Operating Activities—Net Cash Flow	627.600	(342.700)	38.000	149.785	212.576
INVESTING ACTIVITIES					
Short-Term Investments—Change	652.300	(516.600)	(279.200)	174.254	(76.309)
Capital Expenditures	536.800	506.000	425.800	244.375	188.171
Sale of Property, Plant, and Equipment	98.700	88.900	41.300	60.220	0.000
Acquisitions	2,458.700	0.000	124.700	174.885	0.000
Investing Activities—Other	(233.900)	(1,133.000)	(31.000)	(14.394)	16.637
Investing Activities—Net Cash Flow	(2,478.400)	(2,066.700)	(819.400)	(199.180)	(247.843)
FINANCING ACTIVITIES					
Sale of Common and Preferred Stock	1,479.100	133.100	1,125.400	50.328	38.078
Cash Dividends	0.000	1.400	0.000	0.000	0.000
Long-Term Debt—Issuance	1,540.700	2,296.300	732.100	0.000	0.000
Long-Term Debt—Reduction	18.300	0.800	1.200	1.205	3.079
Current Debt—Changes	(52.300)	16.900	21.400	0.000	0.000
Financing Activities—Other	20.600	29.900	(0.500)	(2.184)	0.000
Financing Activities—Net Cash Flow	20.600	29.900	(0.500)	46.939	34.999
Exchange Rate Effect	(112.100)	(6.500)	4.600	2.611	(3.489)
Cash and Equivalents—Change	1,006.900	58.100	1,100.400	0.155	(3.757)
DIRECT OPERATING ACTIVITIES					
Interest Paid—Net	11.000	17.600	26.400	24.999	38.306
Income Taxes Paid	151.400	135.700	9.500	75.817	93.420

COMPUTATIONAL EXERCISES

The Arithmetic of Growth Valuations

Using a simple framework we call "the arithmetic of growth valuations," we explore the consequences for the owner's wealth of changes in expectations regarding the corporation's earnings growth. We provide four numerical examples to illustrate this point. The reader will be well served by coming back to these simple examples and work through the consequences of the strategies and schemes presented throughout the book.

Case 1

A corporation is currently reporting annual net earnings of $30.0 million. Assume that five years from now, when its growth has leveled off somewhat, the corporation will be valued at 15 times earnings.

Further assume that the company will pay no dividends over the next five years and that investors in growth stocks currently seek returns of 25% (before considering capital gains taxes). Suppose the corporation's earnings have been growing at a 15% annual rate and appear likely to continue increasing at the same rate over the next five years.

At the end of that period, earnings (rounded) will be $_____ million annually. Applying a multiple of 15 times to that figure produces a valuation at the end of the fifth year of $_____ million. Investors seeking a 25% rate of return will pay $_____ million today for that future value.

Say the founder still owns 20% of the shares outstanding, which means she is worth $_____ million. Suppose investors conclude for some reason that the corporation's potential for increasing its earnings has changed from 15% to 25% per annum.

The value of corporation's shares will change from $_____ million to $_____ million, keeping previous assumptions intact. Now the founder's shares are worth $_____ million, a difference of $_____ .

Case 2

A corporation is currently reporting annual net earnings of $20.0 million. Assume that five years from now, when its growth has leveled off somewhat, the corporation will be valued at 20 times earnings.

Further assume that the company will pay no dividends over the next five years and that investors in growth stocks currently seek returns of 22% (before considering capital gains taxes). Suppose the corporation's earnings have been growing at a 20% annual rate and appear likely to continue increasing at the same rate over the next five years.

At the end of that period, earnings (rounded) will be $_____ million annually. Applying a multiple of 20 times to that figure produces a valuation at the end of the fifth year of $_____ million. Investors seeking a 22% rate of return will pay $_____ million today for that future value.

Say the founder still owns 40% of the shares outstanding, which means she is worth $_____ million. Suppose investors conclude for some reason that the corporation's potential for increasing its earnings has changed from 20% to 18% per annum.

The value of corporation's shares will change from $_____ million to $_____ million, keeping previous assumptions intact. Now the founder's shares are worth $_____ million, a difference of $_____ .

Case 3

A corporation is currently reporting annual net earnings of $20.0 million. Assume that five years from now, when its growth has leveled off somewhat, the corporation will be valued at 12 times earnings.

Further assume that the company will pay no dividends over the next five years and that investors in growth stocks currently seek returns of 25% (before considering capital gains taxes). Suppose the corporation's earnings have been growing at a 10% annual rate and appear likely to continue increasing at the same rate over the next five years.

At the end of that period, earnings (rounded) will be $_____ million annually. Applying a multiple of 12 times

to that figure produces a valuation at the end of the fifth year of
$_____ million. Investors seeking a 25% rate of return will
pay $_____ million today for that future value.

Say the founder still owns 20% of the shares outstanding, which
means she is worth $_____ million. Suppose investors con-
clude for some reason that the corporation's potential for increasing
its earnings has changed from 10% to 20% per annum.

The value of corporation's shares will change from
$_____ million to $_____ million, keeping previous assumptions intact. Now the founder's shares are worth
$_____ million, a difference of $_____ .

Case 4

A corporation is currently reporting annual net earnings of $20.0 mil-
lion. Assume that five years from now, when its growth has leveled
off somewhat, the corporation will be valued at 20 times earnings.

Further assume that the company will pay no dividends over the
next five years and that investors in growth stocks currently seek returns of 22% (before considering capital gains taxes). Suppose the
corporation's earnings have been growing at a 12% annual rate and
appear likely to continue increasing at the same rate over the next
five years.

At the end of that period, earnings (rounded) will be
$_____ million annually. Applying a multiple of 20 times
to that figure produces a valuation at the end of the fifth year of
$_____ million. Investors seeking a 22% rate of return will
pay $_____ million today for that future value.

Say the founder still owns 40% of the shares outstanding, which
means she is worth $_____ million. Suppose investors con-
clude for some reason that the corporation's potential for increasing
its earnings has changed from 12% to 18% per annum.

The value of corporation's shares will change from
$_____ million to $_____ million, keeping previous assumptions intact. Now the founder's shares are worth
$_____ million, a difference of $_____ .

Market Value versus Book Value of Bonds

This is an example of how a liability can be an asset. Long-term bonds, that are carried in the books at face value in the liability side of the balance sheet, are in fact an asset when their market value is above their face value; on the other hand, when the market value of a bond is below its book value, the bonds represent a larger liability than accounted for in the balance sheet.

Case 1

A firm shows in its books bonds with a face value of $20,000,000. The bonds were issued at par, with a semiannual coupon rate of 12.125%, and now have eight years to maturity. However, the bonds are now priced to yield 15.730%. The market value of this long-term obligation is $_____ and the difference between the market value and the book value of the bond is $_____ .

Case 2

A firm shows in its books bonds with a face value of $50,000,000. The bonds were issued at par, with a semi-annual coupon rate of 14.125%, and now have eight years to maturity. However, the bonds are now priced to yield 10.500%. The market value of this long-term obligation is $_____ and the difference between the market value and the book value of the bond is $_____ .

Case 3

A firm shows in its books bonds with a face value of $35,000,000. The bonds were issued at par, with a semi-annual coupon rate of 6.000%, and now have eight years to maturity. However, the bonds are now priced to yield 10.000%. The market value of this long-term obligation is $_____ and the difference between the market value and the book value of the bond is $_____ .

Acquisitions Driven by P/E Multiples

Management can boost sales through techniques that more properly fall into the category of corporate finance. Increasing the rate of revenue increases through mergers and acquisitions is the most common example. A corporation can easily accelerate its sales growth by buying other companies and adding their sales to its own. Creating genuine value for shareholders through acquisitions is more difficult, although unwary investors sometimes fail to recognize the distinction.

In the following fictitious examples, Big Time Corp. is set to acquire Small Change, a smaller, privately owned company in the same industry. What will be the impact of a stock-for-stock transaction on the price-per-share of Big Corp?

Case 1

Big Time Corp.'s sales increase by 10.0% between Year 1 and Year 2. Small Change, a smaller, privately owned company in the same industry, also achieves 10.0% year-over-year sales growth. Suppose now that at the end of Year 1, Big Time acquires Small Change with shares of its own stock. The Big Time income statements under this assumption ("Acquisition Scenario") show a _____ sales increase between Year 1 and Year 2.

On the face of it, a company growing at _____ a year is sexier than one growing at only 10.0% a year. Observe, however, that Big Time's profitability, measured by net income as a percentage of sales, does not improve as a result of the acquisition. Combining two companies with equivalent profit margins of _____ produces a larger company that earns _____ on sales.

If Big Time decides not to acquire Small Change, its number of shares outstanding remains at 125.0 million. The earnings increase from $_____ million in Year 1 to $_____ million in Year 2 raises earnings-per-share from $_____ to $_____. With the price-earnings multiple at_____times, equivalent to the average of the company's industry peers, Big Time's stock price rises from $_____ to $_____ a share.

In the Acquisition Scenario, on the other hand, Big Time pays its industry-average earnings multiple of 12 times for Small Change, for

Acquisitions Driven by P/E Multiples
Big Time Corp. and Small Change Inc

Debt	$ 1,000	32.0
Equity	$ 1,000	25.0
Big Time Annual Coupon Rate for Debt	10%	
Small Change Annual Coupon Rate for Debt	15%	

($000.000) Omitted

	Non-Acquisition Scenario				Acquisition Scenario	
	Big Time Corp		Small Change Inc.		Big Time Corp	
	Year 1	Year 2	Year 1	Year 2	Year 1	Year 2
Sales	$5,000.0		$238.1		$5,000.0	
Cost and Expenses						
Cost of Goods Sold	3,422.7		160.6		$3,422.7	
Selling, General, and Administrative Expenses	1250.0		61.9		$1,250.0	
Interest Expense	100.0		4.8		$100.0	
Total Costs and Expenses	4,772.7		227.3		$4,772.7	
Income before Income Tax Expenses	227.3		10.8		$227.3	
Income Taxes	77.3		3.7		77.3	
Net Income	$ 150.0		$ 7.1		$150.0	
Year-over-Year Sales Increase						
Net Income as a Percentage of Sales	3.0%		3.0%		3.0%	
Shares Outstanding (million)	125.0				125.0	
Earnings per Share						
Price-Earnings Multiple (times)						
Price per Share						
Year-over-Year Increase						
Market Capitalization						
Year-over-Year Increase						
Debt/Equity Ratio						
Acquisition Price						
Number of Shares						

taxrate	34%
growth_rate	10%
industry_PE_mult	12

a total acquisition price of million. At Big Time's Year 1 share price of $_____ , the purchase therefore requires the issuance of million shares.

With the addition of Small Change's net income, Big Time earns $_____ million in Year 2. Dividing that figure by the increased number of shares outstanding (_____ million) produces earnings per share of $_____ . At a price-earnings multiple of 12 times, Big Time is worth $_____ a share, precisely the price calculated in the Non-Acquisition Scenario.

The mere increase in annual sales growth from _____% to _____% has not benefited shareholders, whose shares increase in value by _____% whether Big Time acquires Small Change or not.

Case 2

Big Time Corp.'s sales increase by 8.0% between Year 1 and Year 2. Small Change, a smaller, privately owned company in the same industry, also achieves 8.0% year-over-year sales growth. Suppose now that at the end of Year 1, Big Time acquires Small Change with shares of its own stock. The Big Time income statements under this assumption ("Acquisition Scenario") show a _____% sales increase between Year 1 and Year 2.

On the face of it, a company growing at _____% a year is sexier than one growing at only 8.0% a year. Observe, however, that Big Time's profitability, measured by net income as a percentage of sales, does not improve as a result of the acquisition. Combining two companies with equivalent profit margins of _____% produces a larger company that also earns _____% on sales. Shareholders do not gain anything in the process, as the figures below demonstrate.

If Big Time decides not to acquire Small Change, its number of shares outstanding remains at 125.0 million. The earnings increase from $_____ million in Year 1 to $_____ million in Year 2 raises earnings-per-share from $_____ to $_____ . With the price-earnings multiple at 16 times, equivalent to the average of the company's industry peers, Big Time's stock price rises from $_____ to $_____ a share.

Acquisitions Driven by P/E Multiples
Big Time Corp. and Small Change Inc

Debt		$ 1,000	$ 1,000
Equity		$ 1,000	$ 1,000
Big Time Annual Coupon Rate for Debt	10%	32.0	
Small Change Annual Coupon Rate for Debt	15%	25.0	

($000.000) Omitted

	Non-Acquisition Scenario				Acquisition Scenario	
	Big Time Corp		Small Change Inc.		Big Time Corp	
	Year 1	Year 2	Year 1	Year 2	Year 1	Year 2
Sales	$5,000.0		$238.1		$5,000.0	
Cost and Expenses						
Cost of Goods Sold	3,422.7		160.6		$3,422.7	
Selling, General, and Administrative Expenses	1250.0		61.9		$1,250.0	
Interest Expense	100.0		4.8		$ 100.0	
Total Costs and Expenses	4,772.7		227.3		$4,772.7	
Income before Income Tax Expenses	227.3		10.8		$ 227.3	
Income Taxes	77.3		3.7		77.3	
Net Income	$ 150.0		$ 7.1		$ 150.0	
Year-over-Year Sales Increase						
Net Income as a Percentage of Sales	3.0%		3.0%		3.0%	
Shares Outstanding (million)	125.0				125.0	
Earnings per Share						
Price-Earnings Multiple (times)						
Price per Share						
Year-over-Year Increase						
Market Capitalization						
Year-over-Year Increase						
Debt/Equity Ratio						
Acquisition Price						
Number of Shares						

taxrate	34%
growth_rate	8%
industry_PE_mult	16

   In the Acquisition Scenario, on the other hand, Big Time pays its industry-average earnings multiple of 16 times for Small Change, for a total acquisition price of $_____ million. At Big Time's Year 1 share price of $_____, the purchase therefore requires the issuance of $_____ million shares. With the addition of Small Change's net income, Big Time earns $_____ million in Year 2. Dividing that figure by the increased number of shares outstanding (_____ million) produces earnings per share of $_____. At a price-earnings multiple of 16 times, Big Time is worth $_____ a share, precisely the price calculated in the Non-Acquisition Scenario.

   The mere increase in annual sales growth from 8.0% to _____% has not benefited shareholders, whose shares increase in value by _____% whether Big Time acquires Small Change or not.

Case 3

Big Time Corp.'s sales increase by 16.0% between Year 1 and Year 2. Small Change, a smaller, privately owned company in the same industry, also achieves 16.0% year-over-year sales growth. Suppose now that at the end of Year 1, Big Time acquires Small Change with shares of its own stock. The Big Time income statements under this assumption ("Acquisition Scenario") show a _____% sales increase between Year 1 and Year 2.

   On the face of it, a company growing at _____% a year is sexier than one growing at only 16.0% a year. Observe, however, that Big Time's profitability, measured by net income as a percentage of sales, does not improve as a result of the acquisition. Combining two companies with equivalent profit margins of _____% produces a larger company that also earns _____% on sales. Shareholders do not gain anything in the process, as the figures below demonstrate.

   If Big Time decides not to acquire Small Change, its number of shares outstanding remains at 125.0 million. The earnings increase from $_____ million in Year 1 to $_____ million in Year 2 raises earnings-per-share from $_____ to $_____. With the price-earnings multiple at 24 times,

Acquisitions Driven by P/E Multiples
Big Time Corp. and Small Change Inc

Debt	$ 1,000	32.0	$ 1,000
Equity	$ 1,000	25.0	$ 1,000
Big Time Annual Coupon Rate for Debt	10%		
Small Change Annual Coupon Rate for Debt	15%		

($000.000) Omitted

	Non-Acquisition Scenario				Acquisition Scenario	
	Big Time Corp		Small Change Inc.		Big Time Corp	
	Year 1	Year 2	Year 1	Year 2	Year 1	Year 2
Sales	$5,000.0		$238.1		$5,000.0	
Cost and Expenses						
Cost of Goods Sold	3,422.7		160.6		$3,422.7	
Selling, General, and Administrative Expenses	1250.0		61.9		$1,250.0	
Interest Expense	100.0		4.8		$ 100.0	
Total Costs and Expenses	4,772.7		227.3		$4,772.7	
Income before Income Tax Expenses	227.3		10.8		$ 227.3	
Income Taxes	77.3		3.7		77.3	
Net Income	$ 150.0		$ 7.1		$ 150.0	
Year-over-Year Sales Increase						
Net Income as a Percentage of Sales	3.0%		3.0%		3.0%	
Shares Outstanding (million)	125.0				125.0	
Earnings per Share						
Price-Earnings Multiple (times)						
Price per Share						
Year-over-Year Increase						
Market Capitalization						
Year-over-Year Increase						
Debt/Equity Ratio						
Acquisition Price						
Number of Shares						

taxrate	34%
growth_rate	16%
industry_PE_mult	24

equivalent to the average of the company's industry peers, Big Time's stock price rises from $_____ to $_____ a share.

In the Acquisition Scenario, on the other hand, Big Time pays its industry-average earnings multiple of 24 times for Small Change, for a total acquisition price of million. At Big Time's Year 1 share price of $_____, the purchase therefore requires the issuance of million shares. With the addition of Small Change's net income, Big Time earns $_____ million in Year 2. Dividing that figure by the increased number of shares outstanding (_____ million) produces earnings per share of $_____. At a price-earnings multiple of 24 times, Big Time is worth $_____ a share, precisely the price calculated in the Non-Acquisition Scenario.

The mere increase in annual sales growth from 16.0% to _____% has not benefited shareholders, whose shares increase in value by _____% whether Big Time acquires Small Change or not.

Stock Prices and Goodwill

Including goodwill in the calculations of the ratio of Total Assets to Total Liabilities can distort the economic reality of the consequences of acquisitions.

Case 1

The shares of Amalgamator and Consolidator are both trading at multiples of 2.5 times book value per share. Shareholders' equity is $200 million at Amalgamator and $60 million at Consolidator. Amalgamator uses stock held in its treasury to acquire Consolidator for $ _____ million.

The purchase price represents a premium of 75% above the prevailing market price. Prior to the acquisition, Amalgamator's ratio of total assets to total liabilities is _____ times, while the comparable figure for Consolidator is _____ times.

The total-assets-to-total-liabilities ratio after the deal is _____ times. By paying a premium to Consolidator's tangible asset value, Amalgamator creates $_____ million of goodwill.

	United Amalgamators Corporation	United Consolidators Inc.	Purchase Price	Combined Companies Pro Forma		
Case 1						
Tangible Assets	1000	400		1400		
Intangible Assets (Goodwill)	0	0				
Total Assets	1000	400		1603		
Liabilities	800	340		1140	Premium	75%
Stockholder Equity (SE)	200	60				
Total Liabilities and Shareholders' Equity	1000	400		1603	Multiple	2.5
Total Assets/Total Liabilities						
Tangible Assets/Total Liabilities						
Market Capitalization						
Case 2						
Tangible Assets	1000	400		1400		
Intangible Assets (Goodwill)	0	0				
Total Assets	1000	400		1813	Premium	75%
Liabilities	800	340		1140		
Shareholders' Equity (SE)	200	60				
Total Liabilities and SE	1000	400		1813	Rally Multiple	4.5
Total Assets/Total Liabilities						
Tangible Assets/Total Liabilities						
Market Capitalization						

*Ignores possible impact of EPS dilution

Case 2

As the scene opens, an explosive stock market rally has driven up both companies' shares to 4.5 times book value. The ratio of total assets to total liabilities, however, remains at _____ times for Amalgamator and _____ times for Consolidator. As in Case 1, Amalgamator pays a premium of 75.% above the prevailing market price to acquire Consolidator.

The premium is calculated on a higher market capitalization, however. Consequently, the purchase price rises from $_____ million to $_____ million. Instead of creating $_____ million of goodwill, the acquisition gives rise to a $_____ million intangible asset. Somehow, putting together a company boasting a _____ times ratio with another sporting a _____ times ratio has produced an entity with a ratio of _____ times.

Now, let us exclude goodwill in calculating the ratio of assets to liabilities. Amalgamator's ratio of tangible assets to total liabilities following its acquisition of Consolidator is _____ times in both Case 1 and Case 2. This is the outcome that best reflects economic reality.

Case 3

The shares of Amalgamator and Consolidator are both trading at multiples of 1.5 times book value per share. Shareholders' equity is $400 million at Amalgamator and $260 million at Consolidator. Amalgamator uses stock held in its treasury to acquire Consolidator for _____ million.

The purchase price represents a premium of 35.00% above the prevailing market price. Prior to the acquisition, Amalgamator's ratio of total assets to total liabilities is _____ times, while the comparable figure for Consolidator is _____ times.

The total-assets-to-total-liabilities ratio after the deal is _____ times. By paying a premium to Consolidator's tangible asset value, Amalgamator creates $_____ million of goodwill.

Case 4

As the scene opens, an explosive stock market rally has driven up both companies' shares to 3.5 times book value. The ratio of total

	United Amalgamators Corporation	United Consolidators Inc.	Purchase Price	Combined Companies Pro Forma		
Case 3						
Tangible Assets	1200	600		1800		
Intangible Assets (Goodwill)	0	0				
Total Assets	1200	600		2067		
Liabilities	800	340		1140	Premium	35%
Shareholders' Equity (SE)	400	260				
Total Liabilities and SE	1200	600		2067	Multiple	1.5
Total Assets/Total Liabilities						
Tangible Assets/Total Liabilities						
Market Capitalization						
Case 4						
Tangible Assets	1200	600		1800		
Intangible Assets (Goodwill)	0	0				
Total Assets	1200	600		2769		
Liabilities	800	340		1140	Premium	35%
Shareholders' Equity (SE)	400	260				
Total Liabilities and SE	1200	600		2769	Rally Multiple	3.5
Total Assets/Total Liabilities						
Tangible Assets/Total Liabilities						
Market Capitalization						

*Ignores possible impact of EPS dilution

assets to total liabilities, however, remains at _____ times for Amalgamator and _____ times for Consolidator. As in Case 3, Amalgamator pays a premium of 35.00% above the prevailing market price to acquire Consolidator.

The premium is calculated on a higher market capitalization, however. Consequently, the purchase price rises from $_____ million to $_____ million. Instead of creating $267 million of goodwill, the acquisition gives rise to a $_____ million intangible asset. Somehow, putting together a company boasting a times ratio with another sporting a _____ times ratio has produced an entity with a ratio of _____ times.

Now, let us exclude goodwill in calculating the ratio of assets to liabilities. Amalgamator's ratio of tangible assets to total liabilities following its acquisition of Consolidator is _____ times in both Case 3 and Case 4. This is the outcome that best reflects economic reality.

Projecting Interest Expense

For the following three examples, calculate the embedded cost of Long-Term Debt.

Colossal Chemical Corporation

($000,000 omitted)

Long-Term Debt (Excluding Current Maturities)			2001	2002
Notes Payable due dates		Rate		
	2003	12.00%	82	44
	2004	7.50%	56	80
Debentures due dates				
	2009	12.50%	55	55
	2011	10.875%	120	120
Industrial Development Bonds				
	2014	5.875%	40	40
			$353	$339

($000,000 omitted)

2001 Amount	2002 Amount	÷2	=	Average Amount Outstanding	@Rate	=	Estimated Interest Charges on Long-Term Debt
_____	_____	+2	=	_____	_____%	=	$_____
_____	_____	2	=	_____	_____%	=	$_____
_____	_____	2	=	_____	_____%	=	$_____
_____	_____	2	=	_____	_____%	=	$_____
_____	_____	2	=	_____	_____%	=	$_____
Total				_____			$_____

Interest Charges on Long-Term Debt		Average Amount of Total Long-Term Debt Outstanding		Embedded Cost of Long-Term Debt
$_____	÷	$_____	=	_____%

Colossal Chemical Corporation

($000,000 omitted)

Long-Term Debt (Excluding Current Maturities)			Rate	2001	2002
Notes Payable due dates			Rate		
		2003	9.50%	96	65
		2004	9.75%	65	90
Debentures due dates					
		2009	11.875%	50	60
		2011	12.125%	90	90
Industrial Development Bonds					
		2014	5.125%	60	60
				$361	$365

($000,000 omitted)

2001 Amount	2002 Amount	÷2	=	Average Amount Outstanding	@Rate	=	Estimated Interest Charges on Long-Term Debt
_____	_____	+2	=	_____	_____%	=	$_____
_____	_____	2	=	_____	_____%	=	$_____
_____	_____	2	=	_____	_____%	=	$_____
_____	_____	2	=	_____	_____%	=	$_____
_____	_____	2	=	_____	_____%	=	$_____
Total				_____			$_____

Interest Charges on Long-Term Debt		Average Amount of Total Long-Term Debt Outstanding		Embedded Cost of Long-Term Debt
$_____	÷	$_____	=	_____%

Colossal Chemical Corporation

($000,000 omitted)

Long-Term Debt (Excluding Current Maturities)				2001	2002
Notes Payable due dates			Rate		
	2003		6.600%	55	75
	2004		5.750%	40	60
Debentures due dates					
	2009		10.25%	90	90
	2011		9.125%	75	75
Industrial Development Bonds					
	2014		8.500%	80	80
				$340	$380

($000,000 omitted)

2001 Amount	2002 Amount	÷2	=	Average Amount Outstanding	@Rate	=	Estimated Interest Charges on Long-Term Debt
_____	_____	+2	=	_____	_____%	=	$_____
_____	_____	2	=	_____	_____%	=	$_____
_____	_____	2	=	_____	_____%	=	$_____
_____	_____	2	=	_____	_____%	=	$_____
_____	_____	2	=	_____	_____%	=	$_____
Total				_____			$_____

Interest Charges on Long-Term Debt		Average Amount of Total Long-Term Debt Outstanding		Embedded Cost of Long-Term Debt
$_____	÷	$_____	=	_____%

Sensitivity Analysis in Forecasting Financial Statements

1. Given the base case below, calculate the independent effects of a 1% increase in Gross Margin, a 1% decline in the tax rate, and a 5% increase in Sales.

2. Using the same case, calculate the independent effects of a 2% increase in Gross Margin, a 2% decline in the tax rate, and a 5% decrease in Sales.

3. Using the same case, calculate the composite effects of a 5% increase in Sales, a 2% decline in Gross Margin, a 5% increase is SG&A as percent of Sales, and a 2% decline in the tax rate.

Impact of Changes in Selected Assumptions on Projected Income Statement	
Colossal Chemical Corporation **Year Ended December 31, 2002** **($000,000 omitted)**	
	Base *Case*
Sales	$2,110
Cost of Goods Sold	1,161
Selling, General, and Administrative Expense	$528
Depreciation	121
Research and Development	84
Total Costs and Expenses	1,893
Operating Income	$217
Interest Expense	34
Interest (income)	−5
Earnings before Income Taxes	$188
Provision for Income Taxes	$64
Net Income	$124

Note: Use this chart when calculating Cases 1 through 3.

4. Given the base case below, calculate the independent effects of a 1% increase in Gross Margin, a 1% decline in the tax rate, and a 5% increase in Sales.

5. Using the same case, calculate the composite effects of a 5% increase in Sales, a 2% decline in Gross Margin, a 5% increase is SG&A as percent of Sales, and a 2% decline in the tax rate.

Impact of Changes in Selected Assumptions on Projected Income Statement	
Colossal Chemical Corporation Year Ended December 31, 2002 ($000,000 omitted)	
	Base Case
Sales	$2,110
Cost of Goods Sold	1,477
Selling, General, and Administrative Expense	$253
Depreciation	121
Research and Development	84
Total Costs and Expenses	1,935
Operating Income	$175
Interest Expense	34
Interest (income)	−5
Earnings before Income Taxes	$146
Provision for Income Taxes	$50
Net Income	$96

Note: Use this chart when calculating Cases 4 and 5.

PART TWO

Answers

ANSWERS TO QUESTIONS ON EACH CHAPTER

Chapter 1: The Adversarial Nature of Financial Reporting

1. Three ways that corporations can use financial reporting to enhance their value are:
   a. **Reduce their cost of capital**
   b. **Improve their credit ratings**
   c. **Increase their price-earnings multiple**

2. Corporations routinely **smooth their earnings** because the appearance of **smooth growth** receives a higher **price-earnings** multiple.

3. The following are some of the powerful limitations to continued growth faced by companies:
   a. **Entry of Competition**
   b. **Increasing Base**
   c. **Market Share Constraints**

4. **Diversification** reached its zenith of popularity during the **"conglomerate"** movement of the 1960s. However, by the 1980s, the stock market had converted the **diversification premium** into a **conglomerate discount.**

5. The surprise element in Manville Corporation's 1982 bankruptcy was, in part, a function of **disclosure.**

6. Some of the stories used to sell stocks to individual investors are:

a. *A new product with unlimited sales potential*
b. A "play" in some current economic trend such as
    i. *Declining interest rates*
    ii. *Step-up in defense spending*
c. *Possible corporate takeovers*

7. The ostensible purpose of financial reporting is *the accurate portrayal* of a corporation's earnings.

8. Over a two-year period, BGT paid L&H $35 million to develop translation software. L&H then bought BGT and the translation product along with it. The net effect was that instead *of booking a $35 million research and development expense,* L&H recognized *$35 million of revenue.*

Chapter 2: The Balance Sheet

1. A study conducted on behalf of Big Five accounting firm Arthur Andersen showed that between *1978* and *1999,* book value fell from *95*% to *71*% of the stock market value of public companies in the United States.

2. In the examples above, there is no accounting event because *no money changes hands.*

3. As in the case of *first-time recognition of goodwill,* the historical cost principle makes comparable companies appear quite dissimilar. The equally large *hidden asset value* of another company with low-cost debt will not be reflected on its balance sheet, simply because *it has never been acquired.*

4. Through stock-for-stock acquisitions, the sharp rise in equity prices during the late 1990s was transformed into *increased balance sheet value,* despite the usual assumption that *fluctuations in a company's stock price do not alter its stated net worth.*

5. A reasonable estimate of a low-profit company's true equity value would be **the amount that produces a return on equity equivalent to the going rate.**

6. Determining the cost of capital is a notoriously controversial subject in the financial field, complicated by **thorny tax considerations** and **risk adjustments.**

7. Instead of striving for theoretical purity on the matter, analysts should adopt a **flexible attitude,** using the measure of equity value **most useful to a particular application.**

8. Users of financial statements can process only **the information they have,** and they do not always have **the information they need.**

9. Where feasible, users of financial statements should also solicit as **much detail as management will disclose** regarding risks not spelled out **in the balance sheet or footnotes.**

Chapter 3 The Income Statement

1. Students of financial statements must keep up with **the innovations** of the past few years in transforming **rising stock value** into **revenues of dubious quality.**

2. Besides facilitating comparisons between a company's present and past results, the **percentage income statement** can highlight important facts **about a company's competitive standing.**

3. The more widely diversified pharmaceutical manufacturers can be expected to have **higher** percentage **product costs,** as well as **lower** percentage **research and development** expenses, than industry peers that focus exclusively on **prescription drugs.**

4. Executives whose bonuses rise **in tandem with earnings-per-share** have a strong incentive not only **share to generate bona**

fide earnings, but also to use *every lawful means of inflating the figures through accounting sleight of hand.*

5. Along with *employee retirement costs,* another major expense category that can be controlled through *assumptions* is *depreciation.*

6. A company knows that creating *more favorable* expectations about *the future* can raise *its stock price* and lower *its borrowing cost.*

7. An extraordinary item is reported on an *after-tax* basis, below the *line of income (or loss)* from continuing operations.

8. In recent years, *restructuring* has become a catchall for charges that companies wish analysts to consider *outside the normal course of business,* but which do not qualify for *below-the-line treatment.*

9. The most dangerous trap that users of financial statements must avoid walking into, however, is inferring that the term *restructuring* connotes *finality.*

10. The purpose of providing pro forma results was to help analysts *to project future financial results* accurately when some event *outside the ordinary course of business* caused *the unadjusted historical results* to convey a misleading impression.

11. Computer software producers got into the act by *omitting amortization of purchased research and development* from the expenses considered in calculating *pro forma earnings.*

12. In fact, analysts who hope to forecast future financial results accurately *must* apply *common sense* and set aside genuinely *out-of-the-ordinary-course-of-business events.*

13. An older, but not obsolete, device for beefing up reported income is *capitalization of selected expenditures.*

14. A corporation can easily accelerate its sales growth by **buying other companies** and **adding their sales to its own acquisitions.** Creating genuine value for shareholders though is more difficult, although unwary investors sometimes fail to recognize the distinction.

15. If Company A generates external growth by acquiring Company B and neither Company A nor its new subsidiary increases its profitability, then **the intrinsic value of** the merged companies is **no greater** than the sum of the two companies' values.

16. As synergies go, projections of economies of scale in combinations of companies **within the same business** tend to be more plausible than economies of scope purportedly available to companies in **tangentially connected** businesses.

17. Professor Beneish's statistical analysis shows that the presence of the following factors increases the probability of earnings manipulation:
    a. **Increasing days sales in receivables**
    b. **Deteriorating gross margins**
    c. **Decreasing rates of depreciation**
    d. **Decreasing asset quality**
    e. **Growing sales**

Chapter 4: The Statement of Cash Flows

1. For financial reporting (as opposed to **tax-accounting**) purposes, a publicly owned company generally seeks to maximize **its reported net income,** which investors use as a basis for valuing its shares.

2. In a classic LBO, a group of investors acquires a business by **putting up a small amount of equity** and **borrowing** the balance.

3. Analysts evaluating the investment merits of the LBO proposal would miss the point if they focused on **earnings** rather than **cash flow.**

4. The essential idea of a **leveraged buyout** is to acquire a business with a sliver of equity and a large amount of **borrowed capital,** and then pay off the debt with **cash generated from operations.**

5. The EBITDA multiple may come down because **potential buyers** perceive that the LBO organizers **scrimped** on capital spending during their stewardship, meaning that **above-average investment in plant and equipment** will be required going forward.

6. The **cash flow statement,** rather than the **income statement,** provides the best information about a highly leveraged firm's financial health.

7. Revenues build gradually during the **start-up** phase, when the company is just **organizing itself** and **launching its products.** Growth and profits accelerate rapidly during the **emerging growth** phase, as the company's products begin to penetrate the market and the **production reaches a profitable scale.** During the **established growth** period, growth in sales and earnings decelerates as the **market nears saturation.** In the **mature industry** phase, sales opportunities are limited to the replacement of products previously sold, plus **new sales derived from growth in the population.** Price competition often intensifies at this stage, as companies **seek sales growth through increased market share.** The **declining industry** stage does not automatically follow maturity, but over long periods some industries do get swept away by **technological change.** Sharply declining sales and earnings, ultimately resulting in **corporate bankruptcies,** characterize industries in decline.

8. **Emerging growth companies** are start-ups that survive long enough to reach the stage of entering the public market.

9. **Mature industry companies,** are past the cash strain faced by growth companies that must fund large **construction** programs.

10. By studying the cash flow statement, an analyst can make informed judgments on such questions as:

a. *How safe (that is, likely to continue being paid) is the company's dividend?*

b. *Could the company fund its needs internally if external sources of capital suddenly become scarce or prohibitively expensive?*

c. *Would the company be able to continue meeting its obligations if its business turned down sharply?*

11. If corporation's financial strain becomes acute, the board of directors may take the comparatively extreme step of *cutting or eliminating the dividend.*

12. A company with a strong balance sheet can fund much of that cash need by increasing its *trade payables* (credit extended by vendors). External financing may be needed, however, if accumulation of unsold goods causes *inventories* to rise disproportionately to *sales.* Similarly, if customers begin paying more slowly than formerly, *receivables* can widen the gap between *working capital requirements* and *trade credit availability.*

13. Overinvestment has unquestionably led, in many industries, to prolonged periods of *excess capacity,* producing in turn chronically *poor profitability.* In retrospect, the firms involved would have served their shareholders better if they had *increased their dividend payouts* or *repurchased stock,* instead of *constructing new plants.*

14. Another less obvious risk of eschewing financial flexibility is the danger of permanently losing *experienced skilled workers* through *temporary layoffs* occasioned by recessions.

15. The cash flow statement is the best tool for measuring *flexibility,* which, contrary to a widely held view, is not merely a security blanket for *squeamish investors.* In the hands of an aggressive but prudent management, a cash flow cushion can enable a company to *sustain essential long-term investment spending* when competitors are forced to cut back.

Chapter 5: What Is Profit?

1. Profitability is a yardstick by which businesspeople can measure their **achievements** and justify **their claims to compensation.**

2. When calculating **bona fide** profits, the analyst must take care to consider only genuine revenues and deduct all relevant costs.

3. There can be no bona fide profit without **an increase in wealth.** Bona fide profits are the only kind of profits **that truly matter** in financial analysis.

4. Merely **circulating funds,** it is clear, does not increase wealth.

5. An essential element of genuinely useful financial statement analysis is: **the willingness to take accounting profits at something other than face value.**

6. The issuer of the statements can **raise** or **lower** its reported earnings simply by using its latitude to assume shorter or longer **average lives for its depreciable assets.**

7. The rate at which the tax code allows owners to write off property overstates **actual wear-and-tear.**

8. In the **broadcasting business,** companies typically record depreciation and amortization expense that far exceeds physical wear-and-tear on assets.

9. In many industries, fixed assets consist mainly of **machines or vehicles that really do diminish in value through use.** The major risk of analytical error does not arise from the possibility that **reported depreciation expense will substantially exceed economic depreciation,** but the reverse.

Chapter 6: Revenue Recognition

1. Many corporations employ **highly aggressive recognition** practices that comply with GAAP yet **distort the underlying economic reality.**

2. Analysts were questioning Informix's **revenue recognition practices;** in particular, when Informix revealed that about $170 million of its 1996 sales to computer makers and **other resellers** represented **software** that had not yet been **resold to final customers.**

3. Some of the reasons software manufacturers defer recognition of revenue are:

   a. **They can expect run-of-the-mill returns of defective items.**

   b. **A reasonably predictable portion of customers will fail to pay their accounts in full.**

   c. **Uncertainty lingers over a sale until the software has been installed at the end user and the end user's staff has been trained in its use.**

   d. **Resellers often have latitude to return products they cannot sell.**

4. Agreements with resellers that:

   a. **Introduce acceptance contingencies**

   b. **Permit resellers to return unsold licenses for refunds**

   c. **Extend payment terms, or**

   d. **Commit the company to assist resellers in reselling the licenses to end-users**

   mean that license revenue from these transactions should not be recorded **at the time product is delivered to resellers;** rather it should instead be recorded at the time **all conditions on the sale lapsed.**

5. The Informix affair teaches analysts not to construe **auditor-certified compliance with GAAP** as an assurance of integrity in financial reporting. **Liberal** reporting differs from fraudulent reporting, in a **legal sense,** but a corporate culture that embraces the former can foster the latter.

6. Staying alert to evidence of flawed, **or possibly fraudulent,** reporting is essential, even when the auditors **put their blessing on the numbers.**

7. In 1994, KnowledgeWare began supplementing its own sales-force's efforts with agreements **to market its products through resellers.** Almost immediately, the company started to encounter difficulties in **collecting receivables generated by the resellers.** In restating the results, management said that it had booked as revenues **certain sales for which collections were not made.**

8. The receivables-related bombshell that KnowledgeWare dropped on August 30, 1994, was telegraphed by **a simple comparison of revenues and receivables** in KnowledgeWare's 10Q for the first fiscal quarter, received by the SEC way back on November 2, 1993.

9. Prior to the change in accounting practice, which FAS 101 made mandatory, Wal-Mart booked layaway sales **as soon as it placed the merchandise on layaway.** Under the new and more conservative method, the company began to recognize the sales **only when customers completed the required payments and took possession of the goods.**

10. As in any sales situation, aggressive pursuit of new business could result in **acceptance of more marginally qualified customers.** On average, the newer members might prove to be **less financially capable** or less committed to physical fitness than **the previous purchasers of financed memberships.**

11. Under GAAP, the general requirement was to spread membership fees **over the full membership period.** If a company offered refunds, it could not **book any of the revenue** until the refund period expired, unless there was **a sufficiently long history** to enable management to estimate **future experience** with reasonable confidence.

12. GAAP addresses the problem through the **percentage-of-completion method,** which permits the company to recognize revenue in **proportion to the amount of work completed,** rather than in line with its billing.

13. The SEC claimed that to inflate revenues and profits, management at Sequoia Systems:

    a. **Booked letters of intent as revenue,**

    b. **Backdated some purchase orders, and**

    c. **Granted customers special terms that Sequoia never disclosed.**

14. Loading the distribution channels consists of **inducing distributors or retailers** to accept larger shipments of goods than **their near-term sales expectations warrant.**

15. Inevitably, the underlying trend of final sales to consumers slows down, at least temporarily. At that point, the manufacturer's growth in reported revenue will maintain its trend only **if its distributors take on even bigger inventories,** relative to their sales. If the distributors balk, **the loading scheme will unravel,** forcing a **sizable write-off** of previously recorded profits.

16. Users of financial statements should not be intimidated by corporate **press releases** that denounce allegedly irresponsible **securities analysts and journalists.**

17. A stock's value is a function of expected **future earnings,** which partly depend on the **popularity of the company's products** vis-à-vis its competitors'.

18. Analysts who strive to go beyond routine **number-crunching** can profit by seeking **independent verification** of corporate disclosure, even when **the auditors** have already placed **their stamp of approval on it.**

19. Grace executives reckoned that with earnings already meeting Wall Street analysts' forecasts, a windfall **would not help** the company's stock price. Such an inference would have been consistent with investors' customary **downplaying of profits and losses** that they perceive to be generated by **one-time events.**

20. According to Michael Jensen: "Tell a manager that he will get a bonus when targets are realized and two things will happen:

    a. *Managers will attempt to set easy targets, and*

    b. *Once these are set, they will do their best to see that they are met even if it damages the company.*

21. According to Jensen, almost every company uses a budget system that **rewards** employees for **lying** and punishes them **for telling the truth.** He proposes reforming the system by severing the link between **budget targets** and **compensation.**

Chapter 7: Expense Recognition

1. Corporate managers are just as creative **in minimizing** and **slowing down** the recognition of **expenses** as they are in maximizing and speeding up the **recognition of revenues.**

2. To attract subscribers, AOL mailed millions of solicitations and, through arrangements with computer manufacturers, gave away free trial subscriptions. The company did not **recognize these costs as incurred.** Instead, AOL **capitalized the expenditures,** and then **amortized them** over periods of 12 to 18 months.

3. AOL precipitated the plunge in its share prices by cutting the price of its online service by 63%. The move represented **a competitive response to rival providers' low rates,** as well as to the migration of **online services to the Internet,** where most information and entertainment was offered to subscribers **at no charge.**

4. Repeating a recurrent theme in the annals of financial reporting controversies, AOL had initially managed to **report net income,** to which investors duly assigned **a price-earnings multiple,** by exploiting the not **yet well defined accounting rules** of a new industry.

5. During 1999, Chairman Louis Gerstner hailed IBM's **"strong expense management"** as a key to its recent earnings improvement.

6. The investigating accountants and lawyers interviewed more than 200 suppliers of Wickes PLC to determine how many **had paid rebates ahead of schedule.** Clearly, outside analysts, working only with **public statements,** could not have pieced together all of the details of the scheme.

7. Rudimentary analysis of Oxford's financial statements provided more than a hint of **the trouble that lay ahead.** Consider the Form 10-Q report for the quarter ended June 30, 1997, the last filed by the company before the October bloodbath. The **statement of cash flows** displayed the classic problem that first gave rise to **cash flow analysis.** Even though **net earnings** for 1997's first half rose by 74.6% over the comparable 1996 period, **cash from operating activities** deteriorated to −$107.3 million from $139.2 million. The bulk of that adverse swing resulted from medical costs payable turning from a large **cash source** to a major **cash use.**

Chapter 8: The Applications and Limitations of EBITDA

1. The impetus for trying to redirect investors' focus to **operating income** or other variants has been **the minimal net profits** recorded by many "new economy" companies.

2. Users of financial statements had discovered certain limitations in net income as a **valuation tool.** They observed that two companies in the same industry could report similar **income,** yet have substantially different **total enterprise values.**

3. Net income is not, to the disappointment of analysts, a standard by which every company's **value and** can be compared.

4. The accounting standards leave companies considerable discretion regarding the **depreciable lives** they assign to their **property, plant, and equipment.** The same applies to amortization schedules for **intangible assets.**

5. For some companies, the sum of net income, income taxes, and interest expense is not equivalent to EBIT, reflecting the presence

of such factors as **extraordinary items and minority interest** below **the pretax income line.**

6. Shifting investors' attention away from traditional fixed-charge coverage and toward **EBITDA coverage of interest** was particularly beneficial during the 1980s, when some buyouts were so **highly leveraged** that **projected EBIT** would not cover pro forma interest expense even in a good year.

7. Capital spending is likely to exceed depreciation over time as the company **expands its productive capacity** to accommodate **rising demand.** Another reason that capital spending may run higher than depreciation is that newly acquired equipment may be **costlier** than the old equipment being written off, as a function of **inflation.**

8. Delaying equipment purchases and repairs that are **needed** but not **urgent,** should inflict no lasting damage on the company's **operations** provided the **profit slump** lasts for only a few quarters.

9. Depreciation is not available as a long-run source of cash for **interest payments.** This was a lesson applicable not only to extremely **leveraged** deals of the 1980s, but also to the more **conservatively** capitalized transactions of later years.

10. Beaver's definition of cash flow was more stringent than **EBITDA** since he did not add back either **taxes** or **interest** to net income.

11. Beaver did not conclude that analysts should rely solely on the **cash-flow-to-debt ratio,** but merely that it was the single best **bankruptcy predictor.**

12. Some investment managers consider that the single ratio of **cash flow** (as they define it) to **fixed charges** predicts bankruptcy better than all of **the rating agencies'** quantitative and qualitative considerations combined.

13. Aside from **seasonal variations,** the amount of working capital needed to run a business represents a fairly constant **percentage** of a company's sales. Therefore, if inventories or receivables **increase** materially as a percentage of sales, analysts should strongly suspect that the earnings are **overstated,** even though management will invariably offer a **more benign** explanation.

14. If a company resorts to stretching out its payables, two other ratios that will send out warning signals are:
    a. **Receivables to sales**
    b. **Inventories to cost of goods sold**

15. Merrill Lynch investment strategist Richard Bernstein points out that **operating** earnings tend to be more stable than **reported** earnings, EBIT tends to be more stable than **operating** earnings, and **EBITDA** tends to be more stable than EBIT.

16. Strategist Bernstein found that by attempting to **filter out the volatility** inherent in companies' earnings, investors reduced the **effectiveness** of their stock selection.

Chapter 9: The Reliability of Disclosure and Audits

1. Fear of the consequences of breaking the law keep corporate managers in line. **Bending** the law is another matter, though, in the minds of many executives. If their bonuses depend on **presenting results in an unfairly favorable light,** they can usually see their way clear to adopting that course.

2. At some point, **resigning the account** becomes a moral imperative, but in the real world, accounting firms must be **pushed rather far to reach that point.**

3. **Fraud** is an unambiguous violation of accounting standards, but audits do not **invariably catch it.**

4. When challenged on inconsistencies in their numbers, companies sometimes **blame error,** rather than any intention to **mislead the users of financial statements.**

5. According to president and chief executive of Trump World's Fair Casino Hotel, the firm's focus in 1999 was threefold:

   a. **To increase our operating margins at each operating entity.**

   b. **To decrease our marketing costs.**

   c. **To increase our cash sales from our non-casino operations.**

6. One source of Sunbeam's supposedly robust 1997 profits, according to the accounting firm that the company's board hired for the review, was an **excessively large restructuring charge** in 1996.

7. Deidra DenDanto, formerly of the accounting firm of **Arthur Andersen,** stated in a memo (which unfortunately never reached the board of Sunbeam) that booking **the bill-and-hold transactions** as sales was **clearly in violation of GAAP.**

8. Abundant evidence has emerged over the years of corporate managers **leaning on auditors** to paint as rosy a picture as possible.

9. According to Wade Meyercord, an outside director of California Micro Devices, who helped to uncover the fraud and took over as chairman, the fakery included **fictitious sales of nonexistent goods to imaginary companies.**

10. In theory, the **audit** committee of the board of directors serves as **an additional line of defense** in the struggle for **candid financial reporting.**

11. Many companies are either **stingy with information** or **slippery about the way they present it.** Rather than laying down the law (or GAAP), the auditors typically wind up **negotiating with management** to arrive at a point where they can convince themselves that **the bare minimum requirements of good practice** have been satisfied.

Chapter 10: Mergers-and-Acquisitions Accounting

1. Choosing a method of accounting for a merger or acquisition does not affect the combined companies' subsequent **competitive strength** or **ability to generate cash.** The discretionary accounting choices can have a **substantial impact,** however, on **reported earnings.**

2. Amortization of goodwill entails **no cash outlay.** Neither does it generate cash **through tax savings,** because it is not **a tax-deductible expense.** The amortization does reduce **reported income.**

3. From a cash flow standpoint, investors are actually better off under the **purchase** method.

4. There are approximately 10 academic studies of the issue, covering periods from the 1960s to the 1990s. The studies consistently found that the **higher** reported earnings generated by **pooling** did not cause the stocks of the acquiring companies' to outperform the stocks of companies employing **the purchase method.**

5. Among technology companies, a popular way to boost earnings in the pooling-of-interests era involved **write-offs in-process research and development** of acquired companies.

6. For example, one M&A-related gambit entails the GAAP-sanctioned use, for financial reporting purposes, of **an acquisition date other than the actual date on which a transaction is consummated.** Typically, companies use this discretion to simplify the closing of their books at month- or quarter-end.

7. There can be no guarantee of loans secured by stock issued in the combination, which would effectively **negate the transfer of risk** implicit in a bona fide **exchange of securities. Reacquisitions** of stock and **special distributions** are likewise prohibited.

Chapter 11: Profits in Pensions

1. Under SFAS No. 87, "Accounting for Pensions," the investment returns on a corporate pension plan's investment portfolio flows into **the sponsoring company's operating income.** Management can elect to **capitalize all** or a portion of the year's net pension benefit (cost) as part of **inventory** and then run it through **cost of goods sold.** Alternatively, the company can recognize the pension-related income by reducing **its selling, general, and administrative expenses.**

2. When projecting IBM's future earnings, it is important to segregate **genuinely business-related income** from **profits on retirement plans.** Otherwise, the analysis will give management **undeserved credit** for a general **rise in stock prices.**

3. Analysts should also note that the accounting rules for pension income allow management, within certain bounds, to **divert earnings** from the **nonoperating** to the **operating category.**

   In principle, one would expect a company to base its assumption on **the long-run rates of return observed in stocks, bonds, and other types of investments.**

4. Management cannot invariably modulate their impact on reported earnings as desired. Among the effects is **the gain or loss** that may arise from **settlement of a pension liability.** Such events may be large enough to **spoil attempts to fine-tune the bottom line.**

Chapter 12: Forecasting Financial Statements

1. It is **future earnings and dividends** that determine the value of a company's stock and the **relative likelihood of future timely payments of debt service** that determines credit quality.

2. The process of financial projections is an extension of **historical patterns** and **relationships,** based on assumptions about future **economic conditions, market behavior,** and **managerial action.**

3. Sales projections for the company's business can be developed with the help of such sources as **trade publications, trade associations,** and firms that sell **econometric forecasting** models.

4. Basic industries such as **chemicals, paper,** and **capital goods** tend to lend themselves best to the **macroeconomic-based approach** described here. In technology-driven industries and "hits-driven" businesses such as **motion pictures** and **toys,** the connection between **sales** and the **general economic trend** will tend to be looser.

5. The expected intensity of industry competition, which affects a company's **ability to pass cost increases** on to customers or to retain **cost decreases,** influences the **gross margin** forecast.

6. Since the segment information in may show only operating income, and not **gross margin,** the analyst must add **segment depreciation** to operating income, then make assumptions about the allocation of **selling, general, and administrative expense** and **research and development** expense by segment.

7. The R&D percentage may change if, for example, the company **makes a sizable acquisition** in an industry that is either significantly more, or significantly less, **research-intensive** than its existing operations.

8. The key to the forecasting interest expense method employed here is to estimate the firm's embedded cost of debt, that is, the **weighted average interest rate** on the company's **existing long-term debt.**

9. Accurately projecting interest expense for **highly leveraged** companies is important because **their financial viability** may depend on the size of **the interest expense "nut"** they must cover each quarter.

10. The completed income statement projection supplies **the first two lines** of the projected statement of cash flows.

11. Before assuming a constant-percentage relationship, the analyst must verify that *the most recent year's ratios are representative of experience over several years.*

12. A sizable *net cash provision* might be presumed to be directed toward share repurchase, reducing *shareholders' equity,* if management has indicated a desire to *buy stock* >and is *authorized to do so* by its board of directors.

13. Typically, the analyst must modify the underlying *economic* assumptions, and therefore the projections, several times during the year as *business activity* diverges from *forecasted levels.*

14. A firm may have considerable room to cut *its capital spending* in the short run if it suffers a decline in funds provided by *operations.* A projection that ignored this *financial flexibility* could prove overly pessimistic.

15. An interest rate decline will have limited impact on a company for which interest costs represent a *small percentage of expenses.* The impact will be greater on a company with a large interest cost component and with much of its debt at *floating rates.* This assumes the return on the company's assets is *not similarly rate-sensitive.*

16. Analysts are generally not arrogant enough to try to forecast the figures accurately to the first decimal place, that is, to the *hundred-thousands* for a company with revenues in the *hundreds of millions.*

17. It is generally inappropriate to compare a *quarterly income statement* item (EBITDA) with a balance sheet figure, especially in the case of a *highly seasonal* company.

18. It is unwise to base an investment decision on historical statements that antedate a major financial change such as:
    a. *Stock repurchase*
    b. *Write-off*
    c. *Acquiition*
    d. *Divestment.*

19. A pro forma income statement for a single year provides no information about **the historical growth** in sales and earnings of **the subsidiary** that is being spun off.

20. Pro forma adjustments for a divestment do not capture the potential benefits of increased **management focus** on the company's **core operations.**

21. The earnings shown in a merger-related pro forma income statement may be higher than the company can sustain because:
    a. The acquired company's owners may be shrewdly selling out at top dollar, anticipating a **deceleration in earnings growth** that is foreseeable by **industry insiders,** but not to the acquiring corporation's management.
    b. Mergers of companies in the same industry often work out poorly due to **clashes of corporate culture.**
    c. Inappropriately applying **its management style** to an industry with very different requirements.

22. A **fixed-income** investor buying a 30-year bond is certainly interested in the issuer's financial prospects beyond **a 12-month horizon.** Similarly, a substantial percentage of the present value of future dividends represented by a stock's price lies **in years beyond the coming one.**

23. Radical financial restructurings such as **leveraged buyouts, megamergers massive stock,** and **buybacks** necessitate **multi-year** projections.

24. Of the various types of analysis of financial statements, projecting **future results** and **ratios** requires the greatest skill and produces **the most valuable findings.**

25. The lack of **predictable patterns** is what makes financial forecasting so **valuable.** When betting huge sums in the face of **massive uncertainty,** it is essential that investors understand **the odds** as fully as they possibly can.

Chapter 13: Credit Analysis

1. Financial statements tell much about a borrower's **ability** to repay a loan, but disclose little about the equally important **willingness** to repay.

2. If a company is dependent on raw materials provided by a subsidiary, there may be a **reasonable** presumption that it will stand behind the subsidiary's **debt,** even **in the absence of a formal guarantee.**

3. Illiquidity manifests itself as an excess of current **cash payments due,** over **cash currently available.** The **current** ratio gauges the risk of this occurring by comparing the claims against the company that will become payable during **the current operating cycle (current liabilities)** with the assets that are already in the form of cash or that will be converted to cash during **the current operating cycle (current assets).**

4. The greater the amount by which asset values could deteriorate, the greater the **"equity cushion,"** and the greater the creditor's sense of **being protected.** Equity is by definition **total assets** minus **total liabilities.**

5. Aggressive **borrowers** frequently try to satisfy the letter of a **maximum** leverage limit imposed by lenders, without fulfilling the **conservative spirit** behind it.

6. A firm that "zeros out" its **short-term debt** at some point in each operating cycle can legitimately argue that its "true" leverage is represented by the **permanent (long-term) debt** on its balance sheet.

7. Current maturities of long-term debt should enter into the calculation of **total debt,** based on a conservative assumption that the company will replace maturing debt with **new long-term borrowings.**

8. Exposure to interest rate fluctuations can also arise from long-term **floating-rate debt.** Companies can limit this risk by using **financial derivatives.**

9. Public financial statements typically provide **only general** information about the extent to which the issuer has **limited** its exposure to interest rate fluctuations through **derivatives.**

10. Analysts should remember that the ultimate objective is not to **calculate ratios** but to **assess credit risk.**

11. In general, the credit analyst must recognize the heightened level of risk implied by the presence of preferred stock in the **capital structure.** One formal way to take this risk into account is to calculate the ratio of **total fixed obligations** to **total capital.**

12. In addition to including capital leases in the total debt calculation, analysts should also take into account the **off-balance-sheet** liabilities represented by contractual payments on **operating leases,** which are reported as **rental expense** in the **Notes** to Financial Statements.

13. A corporation can employ leverage yet avoid showing debt on its consolidated balance sheet by **entering joint ventures** or forming **partially owned subsidiaries.**

14. Under SFAS **87,** balance sheet recognition is now given to pension liabilities related to employees' service to date. Similarly, SFAS **87** requires recognition of postretirement health care benefits as an on-balance sheet liability.

15. The precise formula for **calculating** a ratio is less important than the assurance that it is **calculated consistently** for all companies being evaluated.

16. In general, credit analysts should assume that the achievement of **higher** bond ratings is a **secondary** goal of corporate management.

17. The contemporary view is that profits are ultimately what sustain **liquidity** and **asset values.** High profits keep plenty of cash flowing through the system and confirm the value of productive assets such as **plant** and **equipment.**

18. The cumulative effect of a change in accounting procedures will appear **"below the line,"** or after **income taxes** have already been deducted. The sum of net income and provision for income taxes will then differ from the **pretax income figure** that appears in the income statement.

19. Operating margin shows how well management has run the business **buying and selling** wisely, controlling **selling and administrative expenses** before taking into account financial policies, which largely determine **interest expense,** and **the tax rate,** which is outside management's control.

20. Fixed-charge coverage is an **income-statement** ratio of major interest to credit analysts. It measures the ability of a company's **earnings** to meet the **interest payments** on its debt, the lender's most direct concern. In its simplest form, the fixed-charge coverage ratio indicates the **multiple** by which **operating earnings** suffice to pay **interest charges.**

21. Regardless of whether it is **expensed** or **capitalized,** however, all interest accrued must be covered by **earnings** and should therefore appear in the **denominator** of the fixed-charge coverage calculation.

22. The two complications that arise in connection with incorporating operating lease payments into the fixed-charge coverage calculation are:
    a. **The SEC does not require companies to report rental expense in quarterly statements.**
    b. **Retailers in particular often negotiate leases with rents that are semifixed, tied in part to revenues of the leased stores.**

23. Companies sometimes argue that the denominator of the fixed-charge coverage ratio should include only **net interest** expense, that is, the difference between **interest expense** and income derived from **interest-bearing assets,** generally consisting of marketable securities.

24. Ratios related to sources and uses of funds measure credit quality at the most elemental level—a company's ability to **generate sufficient cash to pay its bills.**

25. Given corporations' general reluctance to sell new equity, a recurrent cash shortfall is likely to be made up with **debt** financing, leading to a rise in **the total-debt-to-total-capital** ratio.

26. A company that suffers a prolonged downtrend in its ratio of **cash flow to capital expenditures** is likely to get more deeply into debt, and therefore become **financially riskier** with each succeeding year.

27. Unlike earnings, **depreciation** is essentially a programmed item, a cash flow assured by the accounting rules. The higher the percentage of cash flow derived from **depreciation,** the higher is the **predictability** of a company's cash flow, and the **less dependent** its financial flexibility on the vagaries of the marketplace.

28. Analysts cannot necessarily assume that all is well simply because capital expenditures consistently exceed depreciation. Among the issues to consider are:

   a. **Persistent inflation means that a nominal dollar spent on plant and equipment today will not buy as much capacity as it did when the depreciating asset was acquired.**

   b. **Technological advances in production processes may mean that the cost in real terms of producing one unit may have declined since the company purchased the equipment now being replaced.**

   c. **Depreciation may be understated, with respect either to wear-and-tear or to obsolescence.**

d. *In a growth industry, a company that fails to expand its capacity at roughly the same rate as its competitors may lose essential economies of scale and fall victim to a shakeout.*

29. A limitation of combination ratios that incorporate balance-sheet figures is that they have little meaning if **calculated for portions of years.**

30. The underlying notion of a turnover ratio is that a company requires a certain level of **receivables** and **inventory** to support a given volume of sales.

31. A **drop in sales** is a possible explanation of declining inventory turnover. In this case, the inventory may not have suffered a severe reduction in value, but there are nevertheless unfavorable implications for **credit quality.** Until the inventory glut can be worked off by **cutting back production** to match the lower **sales volume,** the company may have to borrow to finance its unusually high working capital, thereby increasing its **financial leverage.**

32. Fixed-charge coverage, too, has a weakness, for it is based on **earnings,** which are subject to considerable manipulation.

33. Built from two comparatively hard numbers, the ratio of **total debt** to **cash flow** provides one of the best single measures of **credit quality.**

34. Expected **recoveries** have an important bearing on the decision to **extend** or **deny** credit, as well as on the **valuation** of debt securities.

35. Line of business is another basis for defining **a peer group.**

36. Beyond a certain point, calculating and comparing companies on the basis of **additional** financial ratios contributes little **incremental insight.**

37. **Improving** or **deteriorating** financial ratios can have different implications for different companies.

38. Quantitative models such as Zeta, as well as others that have been devised using various mathematical techniques, have several distinct benefits such as:

    a. ***They are developed by objectively correlating financial variables with defaults.***

    b. ***The record of quantitative models is excellent from the standpoint of classifying as troubled credits most companies that subsequently defaulted.***

    c. ***The scores assigned to nondefaulted companies by these models correlate fairly well with bond ratings.***

39. Like the quantitative models consisting of ***financial ratios,*** the default risk models based on stock prices provide useful, but ***not infallible,*** signals.

Chapter 14: Equity Analysis

1. In this chapter, the discussion focuses primarily on the use of financial statements in ***fundamental analysis.***

2. Of the methods of fundamental common stock analysis, no other approach matches the intuitive appeal of regarding the stock price as the ***discounted value*** of expected ***future*** dividends. This approach is analogous to the ***yield-to-maturity*** calculation for a bond and therefore facilitates the comparison of different ***securities*** of a single ***issuer.***

3. By thinking through the logic of the ***discounting*** method, the analyst will find that value always comes back to ***dividends.***

4. The company's earnings growth rate may diverge from its sales growth due to changes in its ***operating margins.***

5. As a rule, a ***cyclical*** company will not increase its dividend on a regular, annual basis.

6. Many analysts argue that ***cash flow,*** rather than ***earnings,*** is the true determinant of dividend-paying capability.

7. Cash generated from **operations,** which is generally more difficult for companies to manipulate than **earnings,** can legitimately be viewed as the preferred measure of future **dividend-paying capability.**

8. The ability to vary the **discount rate,** and therefore to assign a **lower** or **higher** multiple to a company's earnings, is the equity analyst's defense against earnings **manipulation** by management.

9. It is appropriate to assign an **above-average** discount factor to the earnings of a company that competes against larger, better-capitalized firms. A small company **may also suffer the disadvantages of lack** of depth in management and concentration of **its production in one or two plants.**

10. A building-materials manufacturer may claim to be cushioned against fluctuations in housing starts because of a strong emphasis in its product line on **the remodeling and repair markets**

11. Analysts should be especially wary of companies that have tended to jump on the bandwagon of **"concepts"** associated with the **hot stocks** of the moment.

12. Earnings per share will not grow merely because **sales increase.**

13. Leverage reaches a limit, since lenders will not continue advancing funds beyond a certain point as **financial risk increases.**

14. One way to increase earnings per share is to **reduce the number of shares outstanding.**

15. To the extent that the company funds share buybacks with idle cash, the increase in **earnings per share** is offset by a reduction arising from **forgone income on investments.**

16. Like most ratio analysis, the Du Pont Formula is valuable not only for **the questions it answers** but also for **the new ones it raises.**

17. Besides introducing greater volatility into the **rate of return,** adding debt to the balance sheet demonstrates **no management skill in improving operations.**

18. Some companies have the potential to raise their share prices by **utilizing their assets more efficiently,** while others can increase their value by **increasing their financial leverage.**

19. Management's main adversaries in battles over **"corporate governance"** were aggressive **financial operators.**

20. At least in the early stages, before some raiders became overly aggressive in their financial forecast assumptions, it was feasible to extract value without creating undue bankruptcy risk, simply by **increasing the ratio of debt to equity.**

21. In future bear markets, when stocks again sell at depressed price-earnings multiples, investors will probably renew their focus on **companies' values as LBO candidates.**

22. A leveraged buyout can bring about improved profitability for either of two reasons:
    a. **A change in ownership results in a fresh look at the company's operations.**
    b. **Management may obtain a significantly enlarged stake in the firm's success as the result of the buyout.**

23. Today's **profit improvement** may be a precursor of tomorrow's bankruptcy by a company that has economized its way to **an uncompetitive state.**

24. A focus on **price-earnings** multiples, the best-known form of fundamental analysis, is not the investor's **sole alternative** to relying on technicians' stock charts.

25. For the investor who takes a longer view, **financial statement analysis** provides an invaluable reference point for valuation.

FINANCIAL STATEMENT EXERCISES

1. Indicate in which of the principal financial statements each item appears.

    a.

Item	Balance Sheet	Income Statement	Statement of Cash Flows
Accounts Payable	x		
Accumulated Depreciation	x		
Adjusted Net Income		x	
Capital Expenditures			x
Cash and Equivalents—Change		x	
Common Shares Outstanding	x		
Current Debt—Changes		x	
Direct Operating Activities			x
Earnings per Share (Fully Diluted)		x	
Earnings per Share (Primary)		x	
Equity in Net Loss (Earnings)			x
Extraordinary Items		x	
Financing Activities—Net Cash Flow			x
Gross Plant, Property, and Equipment	x		
Income before Extraordinary Items		x	x
Indirect Operating Activities			x
Interest Paid—Net			x
Investing Activities			x
Investment Tax Credit	x		
Long-Term Debt Due In One Year	x		
Minority Interest	x	x	
Net Receivables	x		
Operating Activities—Net Cash Flow			x
Other Assets and Liabilities—Net Change			x
Other Investments	x		
Preferred Stock—Nonredeemable	x		
Pretax Income		x	
Retained Earnings	x		
Sale of Property, Plant, and Equipment			x
Selling, General, and Administrative Expense		x	
Stock Equivalents		x	
Total Current Assets	x		
Total Income Taxes		x	
Total Preferred Stock	x		

b.

Item	Balance Sheet	Income Statement	Statement of Cash Flows
Accrued Expenses	x		
Adjusted Available for Common		x	
Available for Common		x	
Cash and Equivalents	x		
Common Equity	x		
Cost of Goods Sold		x	
Deferred Taxes	x		x
Dividends per Share		x	
Earnings per Share (Primary)		x	
Equity	x		
Financing Activities			x
Funds from Operations—Other			x
Income Taxes Paid			x
Interest Expense		x	
Inventory—Decrease (Increase)			x
Investing Activities—Other			x
Investments at Equity	x		
Long-Term Debt	x		
Long-Term Debt—Reduction			x
Net Plant, Property, and Equipment	x		
Notes Payable	x		
Other Assets	x		
Other Current Liabilities	x		
Preferred Dividends		x	
Prepaid Expenses	x		
Receivables—Decrease (Increase)			x
Sale of Investments			x
Savings Due to Common		x	
Special Items		x	
Total Assets	x		
Total Equity	x		
Total Liabilities and Equity	x		

C.

Item	Balance Sheet	Income Statement	Statement of Cash Flows
Accounts Payable and Accrued Liabilities—Increase (Decrease)			x
Acquisitions			x
Assets	x		
Capital Surplus	x		
Cash Dividends			x
Common Stock	x		
Deferred Charges	x		
Discontinued Operations		x	
Earnings per Share (Fully Diluted)		x	
EPS from Operations		x	
Exchange Rate Effect			x
Financing Activities—Other			x
Gross Profit		x	
Income Taxes—Accrued—Increase (Decrease)			x
Intangibles	x		
Inventories	x		
Investing Activities—Net Cash Flow			x
Investments—Increase			x
Liabilities	x		
Long-Term Debt—Issuance			x
Minority Interest		x	
Non-Operating Income/Expense		x	
Operating Profit		x	
Other Current Assets	x		
Other Liabilities	x		
Preferred Stock—Redeemable	x		
Purchase of Common and Preferred Stock			x
Sale of Common and Preferred Stock			x
Sales		x	
Short-Term Investments—Change			x
Taxes Payable	x		
Total Current Liabilities	x		
Total Liabilities	x		
Treasury Stock	x		

2. The common form balance sheet.

   Coors, a large beer producer does business the traditional way, Red Hook, a micro brewery also does business the traditional way, while Genesee out sources its brewing, and disposed of large amounts of plant and equipment in 1999/2000.

   Notice the PP&E as a percentage of assets for all three firms in the common size balance sheets below. Genesee is lowest, followed by Coors, and then Red Hook with about 90% of its assets as PP&E.

   Genesee shows a large amount in Cash (probably as a result of Asset Sales in 2000).

   Coors, as a result of being a large, established player, can issue Long-Term Debt, a luxury that is not available to smaller players who must rely on more expensive equity financing. Notice the respective percentages of Total Equity and Long-Term Debt for all three firms.

   Genesee, as a result of its outsourcing strategy must carry proportionally larger amounts of inventory (finished goods) than the other two, which can coordinate better its production and sales, with inventories most likely being raw materials and goods in process.

a. Coors

Common Form Balance Sheet (Percentage)	Dec00	Dec99	Dec98	Dec97	Dec96
ASSETS					
Cash and Equivalents	11.816	17.912	17.543	14.945	8.140
Net Receivables	7.800	10.325	8.668	8.816	8.392
Inventories	6.747	6.936	7.029	7.541	8.886
Other Current Assets	4.188	4.456	4.347	5.325	5.161
Total Current Assets	30.550	39.629	37.587	36.626	30.578
Gross Plant, Property, and Equipment	149.312	150.582	152.658	151.899	156.165
Accumulated Depreciation	104.152	104.410	103.744	99.981	96.416
Net Plant, Property, and Equipment	45.160	46.173	48.914	51.917	59.749
Investments at Equity	3.455	4.475	4.265	3.661	3.493
Other Investments	11.887	0.187	2.153	3.335	0.000
Intangibles	1.807	2.024	1.583	1.620	1.569
Other Assets	7.140	7.513	5.498	2.839	4.610
TOTAL ASSETS	100.000	100.000	100.000	100.000	100.000
LIABILITIES					
Long-Term Debt Due in One Year	0.000	0.000	2.739	1.947	1.248
Accounts Payable	11.422	10.046	9.051	8.064	8.124
Taxes Payable	0.000	0.546	0.694	0.967	0.659
Other Current Liabilities	11.860	14.804	13.802	14.455	11.432
Total Current Liabilities	23.282	25.395	26.285	25.434	21.464
Long-Term Debt	6.444	6.790	7.189	10.269	12.917
Deferred Taxes	5.523	5.091	4.504	5.398	5.584
Other Liabilities	7.524	8.303	8.976	6.738	7.524
TOTAL LIABILITIES	42.774	45.580	46.953	47.838	47.489
EQUITY					
Common Stock	0.602	0.627	0.663	0.689	0.733
Capital Surplus	0.688	0.373	0.719	0.000	2.307
Retained Earnings	55.937	53.419	51.664	51.472	49.471
Common Equity	57.226	54.420	53.047	52.162	52.511
TOTAL EQUITY	57.226	54.420	53.047	52.162	52.511
TOTAL LIABILITIES AND EQUITY	100.000	100.000	100.000	100.000	100.000

b. Genesee

Common Form Balance Sheet (Percentage)	Apr01	Apr00	Apr99	Apr98	Apr97
ASSETS					
Cash and Equivalents	23.637	16.370	9.586	15.119	27.129
Net Receivables	3.857	2.899	7.101	7.495	8.060
Inventories	9.731	9.603	11.402	10.516	10.193
Other Current Assets	6.330	0.182	0.797	1.474	1.445
Total Current Assets	43.555	29.054	28.887	34.604	46.828
Gross Plant, Property, and Equipment	19.907	17.961	86.977	86.962	81.818
Accumulated Depreciation	6.311	4.774	61.246	62.394	57.728
Net Plant, Property, and Equipment	13.596	13.187	25.731	24.568	24.090
Investments at Equity	0.000	0.000	3.712	4.081	3.614
Other Investments	11.365	0.000	19.649	25.546	23.475
Intangibles	28.250	27.839	19.645	7.919	0.000
Deferred Charges	0.000	0.000	0.000	0.000	0.000
Other Assets	3.233	29.920	2.376	3.282	1.993
TOTAL ASSETS	100.000	100.000	100.000	100.000	100.000
LIABILITIES					
Long-Term Debt Due in One Year	1.638	0.313	0.057	0.000	0.000
Notes Payable	0.000	0.000	2.084	0.000	0.000
Accounts Payable	1.423	1.518	5.850	6.164	7.019
Taxes Payable	0.000	0.067	0.844	0.510	0.681
Other Current Liabilities	1.631	3.911	7.616	6.646	6.152
Total Current Liabilities	4.692	5.810	16.451	13.320	13.852
Long-Term Debt	4.999	6.237	3.250	0.000	0.000
Deferred Taxes	0.000	0.398	5.732	6.855	6.419
Minority Interest	0.000	0.000	1.722	1.642	1.234
Other Liabilities	13.274	0.675	10.993	11.716	11.632
TOTAL LIABILITIES	22.965	13.119	38.149	33.534	33.137
EQUITY					
Common Stock	0.953	0.896	0.596	0.633	0.627
Capital Surplus	5.991	6.105	4.068	4.309	4.261
Retained Earnings	71.750	83.431	59.581	64.087	64.536
Less: Treasury Stock	1.659	3.551	2.394	2.563	2.560
Common Equity	77.035	86.881	61.851	66.466	66.863
TOTAL EQUITY	77.035	86.881	61.851	66.466	66.863
TOTAL LIABILITIES AND EQUITY	100.000	100.000	100.000	100.000	100.000

c. Red Hook

Common Form Balance Sheet (Percentage)	Dec00	Dec99	Dec98	Dec97	Dec96
ASSETS					
Cash and Equivalents	8.744	6.229	3.362	0.922	1.222
Net Receivables	1.257	1.340	2.228	2.804	3.823
Inventories	3.184	2.744	2.532	2.910	2.343
Prepaid Expenses	0.000	0.000	0.000	0.235	0.393
Other Current Assets	0.346	0.377	0.340	0.303	0.204
Total Current Assets	13.531	10.690	8.462	7.173	7.985
Gross Plant, Property, and Equipment	103.565	102.492	99.903	101.352	97.053
Accumulated Depreciation	17.521	13.856	10.310	9.627	6.269
Net Plant, Property, and Equipment	86.043	88.636	89.593	91.725	90.785
Deferred Charges	0.000	0.030	0.019	0.058	0.057
Other Assets	0.426	0.644	1.926	1.045	1.173
TOTAL ASSETS	100.000	100.000	100.000	100.000	100.000
LIABILITIES					
Long-Term Debt Due in One Year	0.526	0.513	0.503	0.612	0.140
Accounts Payable	3.111	3.129	2.493	2.366	4.284
Accrued Expenses	2.176	2.253	2.143	1.607	1.668
Other Current Liabilities	2.092	1.791	1.463	1.205	1.000
Total Current Liabilities	7.905	7.686	6.602	5.790	7.092
Long-Term Debt	8.146	8.466	8.796	10.204	6.508
Deferred Taxes	1.490	1.855	2.687	4.121	3.767
Other Liabilities	0.000	0.000	0.000	0.041	0.055
TOTAL LIABILITIES	17.541	18.007	18.086	20.156	17.421
EQUITY					
Preferred Stock—Redeemable	18.804	18.305	17.883	16.499	16.738
Total Preferred Stock	18.804	18.305	17.883	16.499	16.738
Common Stock	0.043	0.043	0.042	0.039	0.040
Capital Surplus	65.880	64.978	63.543	58.703	59.557
Retained Earnings	(2.268)	(1.333)	0.446	4.603	6.243
Common Equity	63.655	63.688	64.031	63.345	65.840
TOTAL EQUITY	82.459	81.993	81.914	79.844	82.579
TOTAL LIABILITIES AND EQUITY	100.000	100.000	100.000	100.000	100.000

3. The common size form of the income statement.

Notice the level of Cost of Goods Sold as a proportion of sales, with Genesee (the outsourcer) showing higher levels of CGS.

Only, Coors, the established player, shows profits for the five years in the analysis. The other two, being new and smaller players, need to spread their fixed costs (including the fixed portion of CGS and SG&A) over smaller volume of sales.

All three firms show low levels of Interest Expense as a proportion of Sales. Although Coors carries Long-Term Debt, its debt service is spread over a much larger amount of Sales.

a. Coors

Common Form Income Statement (Percentage	Dec00	Dec99	Dec98	Dec97	Dec96
Sales	100.000	100.000	100.000	100.000	100.000
Cost of Goods Sold	57.842	53.106	54.912	55.078	57.541
Gross Profit	42.158	46.894	45.088	44.922	42.459
Selling, General, and Administrative Expense	29.935	33.695	32.504	32.132	30.424
Operating Income before Depreciation	12.223	13.199	12.584	12.790	12.035
Depreciation, Depletion, and Amortization	5.355	6.018	6.097	6.430	6.992
Operating Profit	6.869	7.181	6.487	6.360	5.043
Interest Expense	0.266	0.412	0.660	0.848	0.985
Non-Operating Income/Expense	1.048	0.834	1.043	0.821	0.636
Special Items	(0.630)	(0.277)	(1.021)	1.730	(0.366)
Pretax Income	7.021	7.326	5.849	8.062	4.328
Total Income Taxes	2.481	2.839	2.280	3.547	1.821
Income before Extraordinary Items and Discontinued Operations	4.540	4.487	3.568	4.514	2.507
Preferred Dividends	0.000	0.000	0.000	0.000	0.000
Available for Common	4.540	4.487	3.568	4.514	2.507
Adjusted Available for Common	4.540	4.487	3.568	4.514	2.507
Adjusted Net Income	4.540	4.487	3.568	4.514	2.507

b. Genesee

Common Form Income Statement (Percentage)	Apr01	Apr00	Apr99	Apr98	Apr97
Sales	100.000	100.000	100.000	100.000	100.000
Cost of Goods Sold	77.049	80.285	71.329	72.781	72.340
Gross Profit	22.951	19.715	28.671	27.219	27.660
Selling, General, and Administrative Expense	17.583	17.127	24.046	23.587	22.634
Operating Income before Depreciation	5.368	2.588	4.626	3.632	5.026
Depreciation, Depletion, and Amortization	6.466	6.264	4.394	4.079	3.347
Operating Profit	(1.098)	(3.675)	0.232	(0.446)	1.680
Interest Expense	0.907	0.771	0.582	0.000	0.000
Non-Operating Income/Expense	3.071	1.611	4.213	2.467	2.122
Special Items	(3.438)	0.000	0.000	0.000	0.000
Pretax Income	(2.373)	(2.834)	3.863	2.020	3.802
Total Income Taxes	(0.086)	(0.329)	1.397	0.632	1.185
Minority Interest	0.000	0.000	0.825	0.522	0.452
Income before Extraordinary Items and Discontinued Operations	(2.287)	(2.505)	1.642	0.866	2.165
Available for Common	(2.287)	(2.505)	1.642	0.866	2.165
Adjusted Available for Common	(2.287)	(2.505)	1.642	0.866	2.165
Discontinued Operations	(2.901)	(4.960)	0.000	0.000	0.000
Adjusted Net Income	(5.188)	(7.465)	1.642	0.866	2.165

c. Red Hook

Common Form Income Statement (Percentage)	Dec00	Dec99	Dec98	Dec97	Dec96
Sales	100.000	100.000	100.000	100.000	100.000
Cost of Goods Sold	62.013	60.080	63.031	65.811	60.368
Gross Profit	37.987	39.920	36.969	34.189	39.632
Selling, General, and Administrative Expense	34.136	35.069	27.836	29.111	22.011
Operating Income before Depreciation	3.850	4.852	9.133	5.078	17.622
Depreciation, Depletion, and Amortization	9.415	10.160	10.242	9.914	5.726
Operating Profit	(5.565)	(5.308)	(1.109)	(4.836)	11.895
Interest Expense	1.726	1.659	2.080	1.890	0.816
Non-Operating Income/Expense	1.287	(0.149)	0.389	1.059	2.539
Special Items	2.935	0.000	(15.848)	0.000	0.000
Pretax Income	(3.069)	(7.116)	(18.648)	(5.667)	13.619
Total Income Taxes	(0.953)	(2.386)	(6.360)	(1.587)	4.969
Income before Extraordinary Items and Discontinued Operations	(2.116)	(4.731)	(12.288)	(4.080)	8.650
Preferred Dividends	0.000	0.000	0.000	0.000	0.123
Available for Common	(2.116)	(4.731)	(12.288)	(4.080)	8.526
Savings Due to Common Stock Equivalents	0.000	0.000	0.000	0.000	0.123
Adjusted Available for Common	(2.116)	(4.731)	(12.288)	(4.080)	8.650
Adjusted Net Income	(2.116)	(4.731)	(12.288)	(4.080)	8.650

4. For the firms listed, the stage of growth based an analysis of
    their financial statements are:

    a. Remec, Inc. is in the growth stage. Sales are increasing at a
        rapid pace. Operating cash flows are still negligible, and ex-
        ternal financing covers most of the investing, which goes to
        pay for capital expenditures that are much higher than
        depreciation.

Analysis	Dec96	Dec97	Dec98	Dec99	Dec00	Dec01
Market Value	176.900	474.322	416.160	644.793	427.831	@NA
Sales	52.784	118.554	156.057	179.215	189.189	273.499
Operating Income before						
Depreciation	4.532	13.013	24.604	3.964	4.912	17.529
Net Income	1.481	4.972	14.735	(4.831)	(6.675)	10.879
Gross Profit Margin	26.356	30.825	34.209	28.850	30.179	30.019
Return on Assets	5.292	3.964	9.577	(2.210)	(2.981)	2.788
Return on Equity	8.854	4.801	11.467	(2.521)	(3.553)	3.186
Operating Activity—Net Cash Flow	3.386	0.829	0.787	6.263	0.037	10.260
Investing Activity—Net Cash						
Flow-Q	(10.038)	(17.297)	(19.868)	(55.864)	(39.286)	@NA
Financing Activity—Net Cash Flow	(0.096)	70.057	(4.399)	48.434	7.909	132.918
Acquisitions—S&U	0.000	4.012	5.066	0.000	5.825	0.000
Capital Expenditures	3.225	7.363	17.351	18.279	23.199	34.547
Depreciation—Amortization	1.858	3.648	5.381	9.930	11.486	12.416
Issuance of Long-Term Debt	14.600	1.100	12.213	0.000	6.026	0.000
Sale of Common/Preferred Stock	0.067	71.261	2.898	52.676	3.349	138.195
Dividend Payout	3.714	0.000	0.000	0.000	0.000	0.000
Sale of Property, Plant, and						
Equipment	0.000	0.000	0.000	0.000	0.000	0.000
Change in Current Debt	0.000	0.000	0.000	(1.391)	0.000	0.000
Reduction in Long-Term Debt	13.600	3.413	19.510	0.000	1.466	5.277
Deferred Taxes—S&U	(0.611)	(0.767)	(2.408)	1.310	(1.925)	(7.106)
Purchase Common and Preferred						
Stock	0.000	0.000	0.000	2.851	0.000	0.000

b. Hormel is in the mature stage. Sales are increasing, but slowly. Operating cash flows are high, and cover most of investing needs, as well as a large dividend payout. Also, long-term debt is being reduced and no new issues of stock are needed to retire the debt. Capital expenditures are higher than depreciation, but not by much.

Analysis	Dec96	Dec97	Dec98	Dec99	Dec00
Market Value	2,083.081	2,481.697	2,406.994	2,899.081	2,580.848
Sales	3,098.685	3,256.551	3,261.045	3,357.757	3,675.132
Operating Income before Depreciation	164.345	221.095	243.778	305.563	328.493
Net Income	79.408	109.492	139.291	163.438	170.217
Gross Profit Margin	23.982	24.929	28.242	31.053	29.010
Return on Assets	5.529	7.163	8.952	9.696	10.367
Return on Equity	10.109	13.649	17.126	19.430	19.478
Operating Activity—Net Cash Flow	109.408	162.489	229.020	241.701	154.863
Investing Activity—Net Cash Flow-Q	(106.949)	5.026	(49.355)	(37.519)	(41.818)
Financing Activity—Net Cash Flow	39.847	(19.055)	(113.114)	(111.028)	(164.512)
Acquisitions—S&U	12.845	0.140	0.000	0.000	0.000
Capital Expenditures	122.942	116.381	75.774	79.121	100.125
Depreciation—Amortization	42.699	52.925	60.273	64.656	65.886
Issuance of Long-Term Debt	110.553	77.625	17.589	26.100	4.439
Sale of Common/Preferred Stock	0.000	0.000	0.000	0.000	0.000
Dividend Payout	58.056	43.425	34.082	29.360	28.803
Sale of Property, Plant, and Equipment	5.410	4.163	39.792	1.155	3.866
Change in Current Debt	0.000	0.000	0.000	0.000	0.000
Reduction in Long-Term Debt	3.393	4.349	4.312	4.778	43.183
Deferred Taxes—S&U	(2.347)	(0.444)	4.516	1.968	7.160
Purchase Common and Preferred Stock	23.966	45.457	80.076	87.636	75.330

c. Diametrics is in the startup stage. Sales are increasing at an increasing rate, but operating income, as well as operating cash flows are negative. Investing activities are financed by issuing stock.

Analysis	Dec96	Dec97	Dec98	Dec99	Dec00
Market Value	66.443	115.484	115.429	218.883	158.418
Sales	3.797	10.434	12.156	18.687	25.258
Operating Income before Depreciation	(19.333)	(15.883)	(13.769)	(7.820)	(0.586)
Net Income	(23.575)	(21.037)	(17.388)	(10.244)	(2.648)
Gross Profit Margin	(70.582)	28.091	32.642	27.458	38.313
Return on Assets	(97.988)	(73.397)	(68.603)	(32.041)	(9.521)
Return on Equity	(271.789)	(160.062)	(152.983)	(74.012)	(18.668)
Operating Activity—Net Cash Flow	(20.340)	(16.578)	(19.420)	(3.046)	(5.410)
Investing Activity—Net Cash Flow-Q	19.787	(7.757)	3.185	(9.081)	1.624
Financing Activity—Net Cash Flow	0.279	25.310	16.420	11.751	3.582
Acquisitions—S&U	1.068	0.000	0.000	0.000	0.000
Capital Expenditures	1.597	2.958	2.253	1.689	3.438
Depreciation—Amortization	3.114	4.163	3.147	2.225	2.157
Issuance of Long-Term Debt	0.500	1.058	1.819	0.000	0.116
Sale of Common/Preferred Stock	0.966	25.547	16.519	12.996	3.837
Dividend Payout	0.000	0.000	0.000	0.000	0.000
Sale of Property, Plant, and Equipment	0.102	0.237	0.000	0.945	0.000
Change in Current Debt	(0.108)	0.000	0.000	0.000	0.000
Reduction in Long-Term Debt	1.079	1.295	1.918	1.245	0.371
Deferred Taxes—S&U	0.000	0.000	0.000	0.000	0.000
Purchase Common and Preferred Stock	0.000	0.000	0.000	0.000	0.000

5. Du Pont Analysis

a.

Du Pont Analysis of Food Processing Industry's 2000 Results				
Company Name	Sales-Net	Assets-Total	Net Income (Loss)	Stockholders' Equity
Dean Foods Co.	4,065.636	2,003.542	106.118	657.685
Dreyer's Grand Ice Cream Inc.	1,194.356	468.451	25.378	200.912
Earthgrains Co.	2,039.300	2,339.500	54.500	654.900
Flowers Food Inc.	1,619.980	1,562.646	5.045	502.460
Interstate Bakeries Corp.	3,522.929	1,651.925	89.388	591.677
International Multifoods Corp.	2,384.715	736.207	5.135	255.124
Pro-Fac Cooperative Inc.	1,268.542	1,187.266	16.164	159.843
Quaker Oats Co.	5,041.000	2,418.800	360.600	376.300
Suiza Foods Corp.	5,756.303	3,780.478	118.719	598.832
Tofutti Brands Inc.	13.343	4.813	0.956	3.953
Wrigley (WM) Jr. Co.	2,145.706	1,574.740	328.942	1,132.897

Du Pont Analysis of Food Processing Industry's 2000 Results*							
Company Name	Asset Turnover (x)	×	Return on Sales (%)	=	Return on Assets (%)	×	Financial Leverage (x)	=	Return on Equity

Company Name	Asset Turnover (x)	Return on Sales (%)	Return on Assets (%)	Financial Leverage (x)	Return on Equity
Dean Foods Co.	2.03	2.61%	5.30%	3.05	16.14%
Dreyer's Grand Ice Cream Inc.	2.55	2.12%	5.42%	2.33	12.63%
Earthgrains Co.	0.87	2.67%	2.33%	3.57	8.32%
Flowers Food Inc.	1.04	0.31%	0.32%	3.11	1.00%
Interstate Bakeries Corp.	2.13	2.54%	5.41%	2.79	15.11%
International Multifoods Corp.	3.24	0.22%	0.70%	2.89	2.01%
Pro-Fac Cooperative Inc.	1.07	1.27%	1.36%	7.43	10.11%
Quaker Oats Co.	2.08	7.15%	14.91%	6.43	95.83%
Suiza Foods Corp.	1.52	2.06%	3.14%	6.31	19.83%
Tofutti Brands Inc.	2.77	7.16%	19.86%	1.22	24.18%
Wrigley (WM) Jr. Co.	1.36	15.33%	20.89%	1.39	29.04%

*Calculations are subject to rounding error.

Notice that Toffuti Brands has a great ROE (24.18%); however, this is computed on a very small base Total Assets and Sales-Net is very small. Scale matters.

Quaker Oats has a very large ROE (95%) and it is built around high leverage, and high return on assets and return on sales. High leverage does not help Pro-Fac Cooperative's very low return on assets.

6. American Greetings

Annual Ratio Report (Ratio, except as Noted)	Feb01	Feb00	Feb99	Feb98	Feb97	Feb96
LIQUIDITY						
Current Ratio	1.085	1.890	2.743	1.978	2.270	2.138
Quick Ratio	0.395	0.844	1.282	0.814	0.927	0.846
Working Capital per Share	1.488	8.032	10.539	7.109	7.497	6.912
ACTIVITY						
Inventory Turnover	2.932	2.945	2.641	2.522	2.319	2.236
Receivables Turnover	6.156	5.295	5.772	5.872	5.929	5.909
Total Asset Turnover	0.963	0.881	0.966	1.027	1.044	1.063
PERFORMANCE						
Sales/Net Property, Plant, and Equipment	5.278	4.862	5.073	4.912	4.670	4.550
Sales/Stockholder Equity	2.405	1.737	1.638	1.635	1.587	1.622
PROFITABILITY						
Operating Margin before Depreciation (%)	10.674	13.306	17.825	15.731	15.660	15.864
Operating Margin after Depreciation (%)	6.781	10.348	14.785	12.732	12.673	12.104
Pretax Profit Margin (%)	3.916	6.465	12.767	13.300	11.769	8.737
Net Profit Margin (%)	(3.679)	4.137	8.171	8.645	7.732	5.748
Return on Assets (%)	(3.417)	3.574	7.449	8.858	7.826	5.740
Return on Equity (%)	(8.850)	7.186	13.383	14.130	12.271	9.323
Return on Investment (%)	(6.493)	5.311	9.958	12.723	10.567	7.853
Return on Average Assets (%)	(3.544)	3.646	7.895	8.880	8.070	6.112
Return on Average Equity (%)	(8.060)	6.926	13.390	14.045	12.870	9.616
LEVERAGE						
Interest Coverage before Tax	2.781	5.105	10.602	13.719	9.271	8.205
Interest Coverage after Tax	(0.673)	3.627	7.145	9.267	6.434	5.740
Long-Term Debt/Common Equity (%)	36.299	35.300	34.401	11.061	16.130	18.710
Long-Term Debt/Shareholder Equity (%)	36.299	35.300	34.401	11.061	16.130	18.710
Total Debt/Total Assets (%)	27.987	21.914	19.883	16.238	16.524	17.461
Total Assets/Common Equity	2.590	2.011	1.797	1.595	1.568	1.624
Dividend Payout (%)	(42.523)	56.904	36.585	27.335	30.014	40.126

7. Solectron Corp.

Annual Ratio Report (Ratio, except as Noted)	Aug01	Aug00	Aug99	Aug98	Aug97	Aug96
LIQUIDITY						
Current Ratio	3.237	2.682	3.588	2.245	2.713	3.194
Quick Ratio	1.946	1.424	2.521	1.164	1.658	2.097
Working Capital per Share	9.138	8.944	5.307	2.224	2.033	1.872
ACTIVITY						
Inventory Turnover	4.805	5.182	7.954	7.210	7.323	7.339
Receivables Turnover	8.145	8.661	9.384	9.713	9.724	9.452
Total Asset Turnover	1.604	1.859	2.316	2.481	2.236	2.354
PERFORMANCE						
Sales/Net Property, Plant, and Equipment	14.327	13.085	12.839	11.803	11.320	11.288
Sales/Stockholder Equity	3.629	3.718	3.004	4.477	4.020	4.021
PROFITABILITY						
Operating Margin before Depreciation (%)	5.267	7.027	7.414	8.002	9.339	9.237
Operating Margin after Depreciation (%)	2.399	5.249	5.230	5.654	6.508	6.227
Pretax Profit Margin (%)	(0.844)	5.231	5.152	5.654	6.453	6.144
Net Profit Margin (%)	(0.661)	3.542	3.502	3.760	4.278	4.055
Return on Assets (%)	(0.955)	4.826	6.079	8.248	8.533	7.866
Return on Equity (%)	(2.398)	13.169	10.522	16.831	17.198	16.306
Return on Investment (%)	(1.213)	7.031	7.910	12.689	12.113	10.504
Return on Average Assets (%)	(1.060)	6.584	8.113	9.328	9.566	9.547
Return on Average Equity (%)	(2.759)	15.184	14.790	18.932	19.518	18.444
LEVERAGE						
Interest Coverage before Tax	0.104	11.328	11.889	12.300	9.979	12.059
Interest Coverage after Tax	0.298	7.993	8.403	8.514	6.953	8.299
Long-Term Debt/Common Equity (%)	97.608	87.307	33.031	32.634	41.983	55.230
Long-Term Debt/Shareholder Equity(%)	97.608	87.307	33.031	32.634	41.983	55.230
Total Debt/Total Assets (%)	41.249	32.660	19.526	16.110	20.909	27.615
Total Assets/Common Equity	2.510	2.729	1.731	2.041	2.016	2.073
Dividend Payout (%)	0.000	0.280	0.000	0.000	0.000	0.000

COMPUTATIONAL EXERCISES

The Arithmetic of Growth Valuations

Case 1

A corporation is currently reporting annual net earnings of $30.0 million. Assume that five years from now, when its growth has leveled off somewhat, the corporation will be valued at 15 times earnings.

Further assume that the company will pay no dividends over the next five years and that investors in growth stocks currently seek returns of 25% (before considering capital gains taxes). Suppose the corporation's earnings have been growing at a 15% annual rate and appear likely to continue increasing at the same rate over the next five years.

No dividends for the next five years					
		Year	*Earnings*	*Valuation*	*Present Value*
Current Net Earnings		0	30		
Growth Rate	15%	1	34.5		
Required Rate	25%	2	39.7		
		3	45.6		
		4	52.5		
Multiple	15	5	60.3	905.1107	296.6
Owner's Share	20%				59.3
		Year	*Earnings*	*Valuation*	*Present Value*
Current Net Earnings		0	30		
Growth Rate	25%	1	37.5		
Required Rate	25%	2	46.9		
		3	58.6		
		4	73.2		
Multiple	15	5	91.6	1373.3	450
Owner's Share	20%				90
				Difference	30.7

At the end of that period, earnings (rounded) will be *$60.3* million annually. Applying a multiple of 15 times to that figure produces a valuation at the end of the fifth year of *$905.1* million. Investors seeking a 25% rate of return will pay *$296.6* million today for that future value.

Say the founder still owns 20% of the shares outstanding, which means she is worth *$59.3* million. Suppose investors conclude for some reason that the corporation's potential for increasing its earnings has changed from 15% to 25% per annum.

The value of corporation's shares will change from *$296.6* million to *$450.0* million, keeping previous assumptions intact. Now the founder's shares are worth *$90.0* million, a difference of *$30.7.*

Case 2

A corporation is currently reporting annual net earnings of $20.0 million. Assume that five years from now, when its growth has leveled off somewhat, the corporation will be valued at 20 times earnings.

Further assume that the company will pay no dividends over the next five years and that investors in growth stocks currently seek returns of 22% (before considering capital gains taxes). Suppose the corporation's earnings have been growing at a 20% annual rate and appear likely to continue increasing at the same rate over the next five years.

At the end of that period, earnings (rounded) will be *$49.8* million annually. Applying a multiple of 20 times to that figure produces a valuation at the end of the fifth year of *$995.3* million. Investors seeking a 22% rate of return will pay *$368.3* million today for that future value.

Say the founder still owns 40% of the shares outstanding, which means she is worth *$147.3* million. Suppose investors conclude for some reason that the corporation's potential for increasing its earnings has changed from 20% to 18% per annum.

The value of corporation's shares will change from *$368.3* million to *$338.6* million, keeping previous assumptions intact. Now the founder's shares are worth *$135.4* million, a difference of *$(11.9).*

No dividends for the next five years

		Year	Earnings	Valuation	Present Value
Current Net Earnings		0	20.0		
Growth Rate	20%	1	24.0		
Required Rate	22%	2	28.8		
		3	34.6		
		4	41.5		
Multiple	20	5	49.8	995.3	368.3
Owner's Share	40%				147.3

		Year	Earnings	Valuation	Present Value
Current Net Earnings		0	20.0		
Growth Rate	18%	1	23.6		
Required Rate	22%	2	27.8		
		3	32.9		
		4	38.8		
Multiple	20	5	45.8	915.1	338.6
Owner's Share	40%				135.4
				Difference	−11.9

Case 3

A corporation is currently reporting annual net earnings of $20.0 million. Assume that five years from now, when its growth has leveled off somewhat, the corporation will be valued at 12 times earnings.

Further assume that the company will pay no dividends over the next five years and that investors in growth stocks currently seek returns of 25% (before considering capital gains taxes). Suppose the corporation's earnings have been growing at a 10% annual rate and appear likely to continue increasing at the same rate over the next five years.

At the end of that period, earnings (rounded) will be **$32.2** million annually. Applying a multiple of 12 times to that figure produces a valuation at the end of the fifth year of **$386.5** million. Investors seeking a 25% rate of return will pay *$126.7* million today for that future value.

Say the founder still owns 20% of the shares outstanding, which means she is worth *$25.3* million. Suppose investors conclude for some reason that the corporation's potential for increasing its earnings has changed from 10% to 20% per annum.

The value of corporation's shares will change from *$126.7* million to *$195.7* million, keeping previous assumptions intact. Now the founder's shares are worth *$39.1* million, a difference of *$13.8.*

No dividends for the next five years					
		Year	*Earnings*	*Valuation*	*Present Value*
Current Net Earnings		0	20.0		
Growth Rate	10%	1	22.0		
Required Rate	25%	2	24.2		
		3	26.6		
		4	29.3		
Multiple	12	5	32.2	386.5	126.7
Owner's Share	20%				25.3
		Year	*Earnings*	*Valuation*	*Present Value*
Current Net Earnings		0	20.0		
Growth Rate	20%	1	24.0		
Required Rate	25%	2	28.8		
		3	34.6		
		4	41.5		
Multiple	12	5	49.8	597.2	195.7
Owner's Share	20%				39.1
				Difference	13.8

Case 4

A corporation is currently reporting annual net earnings of $20.0 million. Assume that five years from now, when its growth has leveled off somewhat, the corporation will be valued at 20 times earnings.

Further assume that the company will pay no dividends over the next five years and that investors in growth stocks currently seek returns of 22% (before considering capital gains taxes). Suppose the corporation's earnings have been growing at a 12% annual rate and appear likely to continue increasing at the same rate over the next five years.

At the end of that period, earnings (rounded) will be *$35.2* million annually. Applying a multiple of 20 times to that figure produces a valuation at the end of the fifth year of *$704.9* million. Investors

No dividends for the next five years					
		Year	*Earnings*	*Valuation*	*Present Value*
Current Net Earnings		0	20.0		
Growth Rate	12%	1	22.4		
Required Rate	22%	2	25.1		
		3	28.1		
		4	31.5		
Multiple	20	5	35.2	704.9	260.8
Owner's Share	40%				104.3
		Year	*Earnings*	*Valuation*	*Present Value*
Current Net Earnings		0	20.0		
Growth Rate	18%	1	23.6		
Required Rate	22%	2	27.8		
		3	32.9		
		4	38.8		
Multiple	20	5	45.8	915.1	338.6
Owner's Share	40%				135.4
				Difference	31.10

seeking a 22% rate of return will pay **$260.8** million today for that future value.

Say the founder still owns 40% of the shares outstanding, which means she is worth **$104.3** million. Suppose investors conclude for some reason that the corporation's potential for increasing its earnings has changed from 12% to 18% per annum.

The value of corporation's shares will change from **$260.8** million to **$338.6** million, keeping previous assumptions intact. Now the founder's shares are worth **$135.4** million, a difference of **$31.1.**

Market Value versus Book Value of Bonds

This is an example of how a Liability can be an Asset. Long-term bonds, that are carried in the books at face value in the Liability side of the balance sheet, are in fact an asset when the their market value is above the their face value.

Market Value versus Book Value of Debt			Period	Cash Flow	Present Value
Face Value	$20,000,000		0		
Maturity (Years)	8		1	$ 1,212,500	1,124,090
Coupon Rate	12.125%		2	$ 1,212,500	1,042,127
Yield	15.730%		3	$ 1,212,500	966,140
			4	$ 1,212,500	895,694
Price	$16,781,355		5	$ 1,212,500	830,384
			6	$ 1,212,500	769,836
Bond Price =	$16,781,355		7	$ 1,212,500	713,704
Present Value of Coupons		$10,825,540	8	$ 1,212,500	661,664
Present Value of Principal		$5,955,815	9	$ 1,212,500	613,418
		$16,781,355	10	$ 1,212,500	568,691
			11	$ 1,212,500	527,225
Difference	$3,218,645		12	$ 1,212,500	488,782
			13	$ 1,212,500	453,142
			14	$ 1,212,500	420,101
			15	$ 1,212,500	389,470
			16	$ 1,212,500	361,071
			16	$20,000,000	5,955,815
				Bond Price	16,781,355

Case 1

A firm shows in its books bonds with a face value of $20,000,000. The bonds were issued at par, with a semi-annual coupon rate of 12.125%, and now have eight years to maturity. However, the bonds are now priced to yield 15.730%. The market value of this long-term obligation is **$16,781,355** and the difference between the market value and the book value of the bond is **$3,218,645.**

Case 2

A firm shows in its books bonds with a face value of $50,000,000. The bonds were issued at par, with a semi-annual coupon rate of 14.125%, and now have eight years to maturity. However, the bonds are now priced to yield 10.500%. The market value of this long-term obligation is **$16,781,355** and the difference between the market value and the book value of the bond is **$(9,649,269).**

Market Value versus Book Value of Debt					
			Period	*Cash Flow*	*Present Value*
Face Value	$50,000,000		0		
Maturity (Years)	8		1	$ 3,531,250	3,355,107
Coupon Rate	14.125%		2	$ 3,531,250	3,187,750
Yield	10.500%		3	$ 3,531,250	3,028,741
			4	$ 3,531,250	2,877,664
Price	**$59,649,269**		5	$ 3,531,250	2,734,122
			6	$ 3,531,250	2,597,741
Bond Price =	$59,649,269		7	$ 3,531,250	2,468,162
Present Value of Coupons		$37,598,876	8	$ 3,531,250	2,345,047
Present Value of Principal		$22,050,393	9	$ 3,531,250	2,228,074
		$59,649,269	10	$ 3,531,250	2,116,934
			11	$ 3,531,250	2,011,339
Difference	**$(9,649,269)**		12	$ 3,531,250	1,911,011
			13	$ 3,531,250	1,815,688
			14	$ 3,531,250	1,725,119
			15	$ 3,531,250	1,639,068
			16	$ 3,531,250	1,557,309
			16	$50,000,000	22,050,393
				Bond Price	59,649,269

Case 3

A firm shows in its books bonds with a face value of $35,000,000. The bonds were issued at par, with a semi-annual coupon rate of 6.000%, and now have eight years to maturity. However, the bonds are now priced to yield 10.000%. The market value of this long-term obligation is **$16,781,355** and the difference between the market value and the book value of the bond is **$7,586,439.**

Market Value versus Book Value of Debt					
			Period	Cash Flow	Present Value
Face Value	$35,000,000		0		
Maturity (Years)	8		1	$ 1,050,000	1,000,000
Coupon Rate	6.000%		2	$ 1,050,000	952,381
Yield	10.000%		3	$ 1,050,000	907,029
			4	$ 1,050,000	863,838
Price	$27,413,561		5	$ 1,050,000	822,702
			6	$ 1,050,000	783,526
Bond Price =	$27,413,561		7	$ 1,050,000	746,215
Present Value of Coupons		$11,379,658	8	$ 1,050,000	710,681
Present Value of Principal		$16,033,903	9	$ 1,050,000	676,839
		$27,413,561	10	$ 1,050,000	644,609
			11	$ 1,050,000	613,913
Difference	$7,586,439		12	$ 1,050,000	584,679
			13	$ 1,050,000	556,837
			14	$ 1,050,000	530,321
			15	$ 1,050,000	505,068
			16	$ 1,050,000	481,017
			16	$35,000,000	16,033,903
				Bond Price	27,413,561

Acquisitions Driven by P/E Multiples

Case 1

Big Time Corp.'s sales increase by 10.0% between Year 1 and Year 2. Small Change, a smaller, privately owned company in the same industry, also achieves 10.0% year-over-year sales growth. Suppose now that at the end of Year 1, Big Time acquires Small Change with shares of its own stock. The Big Time income statements under this assumption ("Acquisition Scenario") show a *15.2%* sales increase between Year 1 and Year 2.

On the face of it, a company growing at *15.2%* a year is sexier than one growing at only 10.0% a year. Observe, however, that Big Time's profitability, measured by net income as a percentage of sales, does not improve as a result of the acquisition. Combining two companies with equivalent profit margins of *3.0%* produces a larger company that also earns *3.0%* on sales. Shareholders do not gain anything in the process, as the figures below demonstrate.

If Big Time decides not to acquire Small Change, its number of shares outstanding remains at 125.0 million. The earnings increase from *$150.0* million in Year 1 to *$165.0* million in Year 2 raises earnings-per-share from *$1.20* to *$1.32.* With the price-earnings multiple at *12* times, equivalent to the average of the company's industry peers, Big Time's stock price rises from *$14.40* to *$15.84* a share.

In the Acquisition Scenario, on the other hand, Big Time pays its industry-average earnings multiple of 12 times for Small Change, for a total acquisition price of million. At Big Time's Year 1 share price of *$14.40,* the purchase therefore requires the issuance of million shares.

With the addition of Small Change's net income, Big Time earns *$172.9* million in Year 2. Dividing that figure by the increased number of shares outstanding (130.9 million) produces earnings per share of *$1.32.* At a price-earnings multiple of 12 times, Big Time is worth *$15.84* a share, precisely the price calculated in the Non-Acquisition Scenario.

The mere increase in annual sales growth from *10.0%* to *15.2%* has not benefited shareholders, whose shares increase in value by *10%* whether Big Time acquires Small Change or not.

Acquisitions Driven by P/E Multiples
Big Time Corp. and Small Change Inc

Debt		$ 1,000	$ 1,100	32.0	$ 35.2	$ 1,000	1,032
Equity		$ 1,000	$ 1,100	25.0	$ 27.5	$ 1,000
Big Time Annual Coupon Rate for Debt	10%
Small Change Annual Coupon Rate for Debt	15%

($000,000) Omitted

| | Non-Acquisition Scenario | | | | Acquisition Scenario | |
	Big Time Corp		Small Change Inc.		Big Time Corp	
	Year 1	Year 2	Year 1	Year 2	Year 1	Year 2
Sales	$5,000.0	$5,500.0	$238.1	$261.9	$5,000.0	$5,761.9
Cost and Expenses						
Cost of Goods Sold	3,422.7	3,765.0	160.6	176.7	$3,422.7	3,941.6
Selling, General, and Administrative Expenses	1250.0	$1,375.0	61.9	68.1	$1,250.0	1443.1
Interest Expense	100.0	110.0	4.8	5.3	$ 100.0	115.3
Total Costs and Expenses	4,772.7	5,250.0	227.3	250.0	$4,772.7	5,500.0
Income before Income Tax Expenses	227.3	250.0	10.8	11.9	227.3	261.9
Income Taxes	77.3	85.0	3.7	4.0	77.3	89.0
Net Income	$ 150.0	$ 165.0	$ 7.1	7.8	$ 150.0	$ 172.9
Year-over-Year Sales Increase		10.0%		10.0%		15.2%
Net Income as a Percentage of Sales	3.0%	3.0%	3.0%	3.0%	3.0%	3.0%
Shares Outstanding (million)	125.0	125.0			125.0	130.9
Earnings per Share	$1.20	$ 1.32			$ 1.20	$ 1.32
Price-Earnings Multiple (times)	12	12	12	12	12	12
Price per Share	$ 14.40	$15.84			$ 14.4	$ 15.84
Year-over-Year Increase		10%				10%
Market Capitalization	$1,800.2	$1,980.2	$ 85.5	$ 94.1	$1,800.2	$2,074.3
Year-over-Year Increase		10%		10%		15%
Debt/Equity Ratio	55.5%	55.5%	37.4%	37.4%	55.5%	49.8%
Acquisition Price					$85.5	
Number of Shares					5.9	

taxrate	34%
growth_rate	10%
industry_PE_mult	12

Case 2

Big Time Corp.'s sales increase by 8.0% between Year 1 and Year 2. Small Change, a smaller, privately owned company in the same industry, also achieves 8.0% year-over-year sales growth. Suppose now that at the end of Year 1, Big Time acquires Small Change with shares of its own stock. The Big Time income statements under this assumption ("Acquisition Scenario") show a *13.1%* sales increase between Year 1 and Year 2.

On the face of it, a company growing at *13.1%* a year is sexier than one growing at only 8.0% a year. Observe, however, that Big Time's profitability, measured by net income as a percentage of sales, does not improve as a result of the acquisition. Combining two companies with equivalent profit margins of *3.0%* produces a larger company that also earns *3.0%* on sales. Shareholders do not gain anything in the process, as the figures below demonstrate.

If Big Time decides not to acquire Small Change, its number of shares outstanding remains at 125.0 million. The earnings increase from *$150.0* million in Year 1 to *$162.0* million in Year 2 raises earnings-per-share from *$1.20* to *$1.30.* With the price-earnings multiple at 12 times, equivalent to the average of the company's industry peers, Big Time's stock price rises from *$19.20* to *$20.74* a share.

In the Acquisition Scenario, on the other hand, Big Time pays its industry-average earnings multiple of 16 times for Small Change, for a total acquisition price of million. At Big Time's Year 1 share price of *$19.20,* the purchase therefore requires the issuance of million shares. With the addition of Small Change's net income, Big Time earns *$169.7* million in Year 2. Dividing that figure by the increased number of shares outstanding (*130.9* million) produces earnings per share of *$1.30.* At a price-earnings multiple of 16 times, Big Time is worth *$20.74* a share, precisely the price calculated in the Non-Acquisition Scenario.

The mere increase in annual sales growth from 8.0% to *13.1%* has not benefited shareholders, whose shares increase in value by *8*% whether Big Time acquires Small Change or not.

Acquisitions Driven by P/E Multiples
Big Time Corp. and Small Change Inc

Debt	$ 1,000	$ 1,080	32.0	$ 34.6	$ 1,000	1,032
Equity	$ 1,000	$ 1,080	25.0	$ 27.0	$ 1,000	1,000
Big Time Annual Coupon Rate for Debt	10%					
Small Change Annual Coupon Rate for Debt	15%					

($000.000 Omitted)

	Non-Acquisition Scenario				Acquisition Scenario	
	Big Time Corp		Small Change Inc.		Big Time Corp	
	Year 1	Year 2	Year 1	Year 2	Year 1	Year 2
Sales	$5,000.0	$5,400.0	$238.1	$257.1	$5,000.0	$5,657.1
Cost and Expenses						
Cost of Goods Sold	3,422.7	3,696.5	160.6	173.4	$3,422.7	3,870.0
Selling, General, and Administrative Expenses	1250.0	$1,350.0	61.9	66.9	$1,250.0	1416.9
Interest Expense	100.0	108.0	4.8	5.2	$ 100.0	113.2
Total Costs and Expenses	4,772.7	5,154.5	227.3	245.5	$4,772.7	5,400.0
Income before Income Tax Expenses	227.3	245.5	10.8	11.7	$227.3	257.1
Income Taxes	77.3	83.5	3.7	4.0	77.3	87.4
Net Income	$ 150.0	$ 162.0	$7.1	7.7	$ 150.0	$ 169.7
Year-over-Year Sales Increase		8.0%		8.0%		13.1%
Net Income as a Percentage of Sales	3.0%	3.0%	3.0%	3.0%	3.0%	3.0%
Shares Outstanding (million)	125.0	125.0			125.0	130.9
Earnings per Share	$ 1.20	$ 1.30			$ 1.2	$ 1.30
Price-Earnings Multiple (times)	16	16	16	16	16	16
Price per Share	$ 19.20	$ 20.74			$19.2	$ 20.74
Year-over-Year Increase		8%				8%
Market Capitalization	$2,400.3	$2,592.3	$114.0	$123.2	$2,400.3	$2,715.5
Year-over-Year Increase		8%		8%		13%
Debt/Equity Ratio	41.7%	41.7%	28.1%	28.1%	41.7%	8.0%
Acquisition Price						$114.0
Number of Shares						5.9

taxrate	34%
growth_rate	8%
industry_PE_mult	16

Case 3

Big Time Corp.'s sales increase by 16.0% between Year 1 and Year 2. Small Change, a smaller, privately owned company in the same industry, also achieves 16.0% year-over-year sales growth. Suppose now that at the end of Year 1, Big Time acquires Small Change with shares of its own stock. The Big Time income statements under this assumption ("Acquisition Scenario") show a *21.5%* sales increase between Year 1 and Year 2.

On the face of it, a company growing at *21.5%* a year is sexier than one growing at only 16.0% a year. Observe, however, that Big Time's profitability, measured by net income as a percentage of sales, does not improve as a result of the acquisition. Combining two companies with equivalent profit margins of *3.0%* produces a larger company that also earns *3.0%* on sales. Shareholders do not gain anything in the process, as the figures below demonstrate.

If Big Time decides not to acquire Small Change, its number of shares outstanding remains at 125.0 million. The earnings increase from *$150.0* million in Year 1 to *$174.0* million in Year 2 raises earnings-per-share from *$1.20* to *$1.39.* With the price-earnings multiple at 24 % times, equivalent to the average of the company's industry peers, Big Time's stock price rises from *$28.80* to *$33.41* a share.

In the Acquisition Scenario, on the other hand, Big Time pays its industry-average earnings multiple of 24 times for Small Change, for a total acquisition price of *$171.1* million. At Big Time's Year 1 share price of *$28.80,* the purchase therefore requires the issuance of *$5.9* million shares. With the addition of Small Change's net income, Big Time earns *$182.3* million in Year 2. Dividing that figure by the increased number of shares outstanding (*130.9* million) produces earnings per share of *$1.39.* At a price-earnings multiple of 24 times, Big Time is worth *$33.41* a share, precisely the price calculated in the Non-Acquisition Scenario.

The mere increase in annual sales growth from 16.0% to 21.5% has not benefited shareholders, whose shares increase in value by *16%* whether Big Time acquires Small Change or not.

Acquisitions Driven by P/E Multiples
Big Time Corp. and Small Change Inc

Debt	$ 1,000	$ 1,160	32.0	$ 37.1	$ 1,000	1,032
Equity	$ 1,000	$ 1,160	25.0	$ 29.0	$ 1,000	
Big Time Annual Coupon Rate for Debt	10%					
Small Change Annual Coupon Rate for Debt	15%					

($000.000 Omitted)

	Non-Acquisition Scenario				Acquisition Scenario	
	Big Time Corp		**Small Change Inc.**		**Big Time Corp**	
	Year 1	Year 2	Year 1	Year 2	Year 1	Year 2
Sales	$5,000.0	$5,800.0	$238.1	$276.2	$5,000.0	$6,076.2
Cost and Expenses						
Cost of Goods Sold	3,422.7	3,970.3	160.6	186.3	$3,422.7	4,156.6
Selling, General, and Administrative Expenses	1250.0	$1,450.0	61.9	71.8	$1,250.0	1521.8
Interest Expense	100.0	116.0	4.8	5.6	$ 100.0	121.6
Total Costs and Expenses	4,772.7	5,536.3	227.3	263.7	$4,772.7	5,800.0
Income before Income Tax Expenses	227.3	263.7	10.8	12.5	$ 227.3	276.2
Income Taxes	77.3	89.6	3.7	4.3	77.3	93.9
Net Income	$ 150.0	$ 174.0	$ 7.1	8.3	$ 150.0	$ 182.3
Year-over-Year Sales Increase		16.0%		16.0%		21.5%
Net Income as a Percentage of Sales	3.0%	3.0%	3.0%	3.0%	3.0%	3.0%
Shares Outstanding (million)	125.0	125.0			125.0	130.9
Earnings per Share	$ 1.20	$ 1.39			$ 1.2	$ 1.39
Price-Earnings Multiple (times)	24	24	24	24	24	24
Price per Share	$ 28.80	$ 33.41			$ 28.8	$ 33.41
Year-over-Year Increase		16%				16%
Market Capitalization	$3,600.4	$4,176.5	$171.1	$198.4	$3,600.4	$4,374.9
Year-over-Year Increase		16%		16%		22%
Debt/Equity Ratio	27.8%	27.8%	18.7%	18.7%	27.8%	23.6%
Acquisition Price					$171.1	
Number of Shares					5.9	

taxrate	34%	
growth_rate	16%	
industry_PE_mult	24	

Stock Prices and Goodwill

Case 1

The shares of Amalgamator and Consolidator are both trading at multiples of 2.5 times book value per share. Shareholders' equity is $200 million at Amalgamators and $60 million at Consolidator. Amalgamator uses stock held in its treasury to acquire Consolidator for *$263* million.

The purchase price represents a premium of 75% above the prevailing market price. Prior to the acquisition, Amalgamator's ratio of total assets to total liabilities is *1.25* times, while the comparable figure for Consolidator is *1.18* times.

The total-assets-to-total-liabilities ratio after the deal is *1.41* times. By paying a premium to Consolidator's tangible asset value, Amalgamator creates *$203* million of goodwill.

Case 2

As the scene opens, an explosive stock market rally has driven up both companies' shares to 4.5 times book value. The ratio of total assets to total liabilities, however, remains at *1.25* times for Amalgamator and *1.18* times for Consolidator. As in Case 1, Amalgamator pays a premium of 75.% above the prevailing market price to acquire Consolidator.

The premium is calculated on a higher market capitalization, however. Consequently, the purchase price rises from *$263* million to *$473* million. Instead of creating *$203* million of goodwill, the acquisition gives rise to a *$413* million intangible asset. Somehow, putting together a company boasting a *1.25* times ratio with another sporting a *1.18* times ratio has produced an entity with a ratio of *1.59* times.

Now, let us exclude goodwill in calculating the ratio of assets to liabilities. Amalgamator's ratio of tangible assets to total liabilities following its acquisition of Consolidator is *1.23* times in both Case 1 and Case 2. This is the outcome that best reflects economic reality.

	United Amalgamators Corporation	United Consolidators Inc.	Purchase Price	Combined Companies Pro Forma		
Case 1						
Tangible Assets	1000	400		1400		
Intangible Assets (Goodwill)	0	0		203		
Total Assets	1000	400		1603		
Liabilities	800	340	263	1140	Premium	75%
Shareholders' Equity (SE)	200	60		463		
Total Liabilities and SE	1000	400		1603		
Total Assets/Total Liabilities	1.25	1.18		1.41	Multiple	2.5
Tangible Assets/Total Liabilities	1.25	1.18		1.23		
Market Capitalization	500	150		1156		
Case 2						
Tangible Assets	1000	400		1400		
Intangible Assets (Goodwill)	0	0		413		
Total Assets	1000	400		1813		
Liabilities	800	340	473	1140	Premium	75%
Shareholders' Equity (SE)	200	60		673		
Total Liabilities and SE	1000	400		1813		
Total Assets/Total Liabilities	1.25	1.18		1.59	Rally Multiple	4.5
Tangible Assets/Total Liabilities	1.25	1.18		1.23		
Market Capitalization	900	270		3026		

*Ignores possible impact of EPS dilution

Case 3

The shares of Amalgamator and Consolidator are both trading at multiples of 1.5 times book value per share. Shareholders' equity is $400 million at Amalgamators and $260 million at Consolidator. Amalgamator uses stock held in its treasury to acquire Consolidator for *$527* million.

The purchase price represents a premium of 35.00% above the prevailing market price. Prior to the acquisition, Amalgamator's ratio of total assets to total liabilities is *1.50* times, while the comparable figure for Consolidator is *1.76* times.

The total-assets-to-total-liabilities ratio after the deal is *1.81* times. By paying a premium to Consolidator's tangible asset value, Amalgamator creates $*267* million of goodwill.

Case 4

As the scene opens, an explosive stock market rally has driven up both companies' shares to 3.5 times book value. The ratio of total assets to total liabilities, however, remains at *1.50* times for Amalgamator and *1.76* times for Consolidator. As in Case 3, Amalgamator pays a premium of 35.00% above the prevailing market price to acquire Consolidator.

The premium is calculated on a higher market capitalization, however. Consequently, the purchase price rises from $*527* million to $*1,229* million. Instead of creating $*267* million of goodwill, the acquisition gives rise to a $*969* million intangible asset. Somehow, putting together a company boasting a *1.50* times ratio with another sporting a *1.76* times ratio has produced an entity with a ratio of *2.43* times.

Now, let us exclude goodwill in calculating the ratio of assets to liabilities. Amalgamator's ratio of tangible assets to total liabilities following its acquisition of Consolidator is *1.58* times in both Case 3 and Case 4. This is the outcome that best reflects economic reality.

	United Amalgamators Corporation	United Consolidators Inc.	Purchase Price	Combined Companies Pro Forma		
Case 3						
Tangible Assets	1200	600		1800		
Intangible Assets (Goodwill)	0	0		266.5		
Total Assets	1200	600		2067	Premium	35%
Liabilities	800	340	527	1140		
Shareholders' Equity (SE)	400	260		927		
Total Liabilities and SE	1200	600		2067	Multiple	1.5
Total Assets/Total Liabilities	1.5	1.76		1.81		
Tangible Assets/Total Liabilities	1.5	1.76		1.58		
Market Capitalization	600	390		1390		
Case 4						
Tangible Assets	1200	600		1800		
Intangible Assets (Goodwill)	0	0		969		
Total Assets	1200	600		2769	Premium	35%
Liabilities	800	340	1229	1140		
Shareholders' Equity (SE)	400	260		1629		
Total Liabilities and SE	1200	600		2769	Rally Multiple	3.5
Total Assets/Total Liabilities	1.5	1.76		2.43		
Tangible Assets/Total Liabilities	1.5	1.76		1.58		
Market Capitalization	1400	910		5700		

*Ignores possible impact of EPS dilution

Projecting Interest Expense

<table>
<tr><td colspan="6">Colossal Chemical Corporation</td></tr>
<tr><td colspan="6">($000,000 omitted)</td></tr>
<tr><td colspan="4">Long-Term Debt
(Excluding Current
Maturitites)</td><td>2001</td><td>2002</td></tr>
<tr><td>Notes Payable due dates</td><td></td><td>Rate</td><td></td><td></td><td></td></tr>
<tr><td></td><td>2003</td><td>12.00%</td><td></td><td>82</td><td>44</td></tr>
<tr><td></td><td>2004</td><td>7.50%</td><td></td><td>56</td><td>80</td></tr>
<tr><td>Debentures due dates</td><td></td><td></td><td></td><td></td><td></td></tr>
<tr><td></td><td>2009</td><td>12.50%</td><td></td><td>55</td><td>55</td></tr>
<tr><td></td><td>2011</td><td>10.875%</td><td></td><td>120</td><td>120</td></tr>
<tr><td>Industrial Development Bonds</td><td></td><td></td><td></td><td></td><td></td></tr>
<tr><td></td><td>2014</td><td>5.875%</td><td></td><td>40</td><td>40</td></tr>
<tr><td></td><td></td><td></td><td></td><td>$353</td><td>$339</td></tr>
</table>

($000,000 omitted)

2001 Amount	2002 Amount	÷ 2	=	Average Amount Outstanding	@Rate	=	Estimated Interest Charges on Long-Term Debt
82	44	2	=	63	12.000%	=	$ 7.560
56	80	2	=	68	7.500%	=	$ 5.100
55	55	2	=	55	12.500%	=	$ 6.875
120	120	2	=	120	10.875%	=	$13.050
40	40	2	=	40	5.875%	=	$ 2.350
Total				346			$34.935

Interest Charges on Long-Term Debt		Average Amount of Total Long-Term Debt Outstanding		Embedded Cost of Long-Term Debt
$34.935	÷	$346	=	10.10%

Colossal Chemical Corporation

($000,000 omitted)

Long-Term Debt (Excluding Current Maturities)				2001	2002
Notes Payable due dates		Rate			
	2003	9.50%		96	65
	2004	9.75%		65	90
Debentures due dates					
	2009	11.875%		50	60
	2011	12.125%		90	90
Industrial Development Bonds					
	2014	5.125%		60	60
				$361	$365

($000,000 omitted)

2001 Amount	2002 Amount	÷2	=	Average Amount Outstanding	@Rate	=	Estimated Interest Charges on Long-Term Debt
96	65	2	=	80.5	9.500%	=	$ 7.648
65	90	2	=	77.5	9.750%	=	$ 7.556
50	60	2	=	55	11.875%	=	$ 6.531
90	90	2	=	90	12.125%	=	$10.913
60	60	2	=	60	5.125%	=	$ 3.075
Total				363			$35.723

Interest Charges on Long-Term Debt		Average Amount of Total Long-Term Debt Outstanding		Embedded Cost of Long-Term Debt
$35.723	÷	$363	=	9.84%

Colossal Chemical Corporation

($000,000 omitted)

Long-Term Debt (Excluding Current Maturities)			*2001*	*2002*
Notes Payable due dates		Rate		
	2003	6.600%	55	75
	2004	5.750%	40	60
Debentures due dates				
	2009	10.25%	90	90
	2011	9.125%	75	75
Industrial Development Bonds				
	2014	8.500%	80	80
			$340	$380

($000,000 omitted)

2001 Amount	*2002 Amount*	*÷2*	*=*	*Average Amount Outstanding*	*@Rate*	*=*	*Estimated Interest Charges on Long-Term Debt*
55	75	2	=	65	6.600%	=	$ 4.290
40	60	2	=	50	5.750%	=	$ 2.875
90	90	2	=	90	10.250%	=	$ 9.225
75	75	2	=	75	9.125%	=	$ 6.844
80	80	2	=	80	8.500%	=	$ 6.800
Total				360			$30.034

Interest Charges on Long-Term Debt		*Average Amount of Total Long-Term Debt Outstanding*		*Embedded Cost of Long-Term Debt*
$30.034	÷	$360	=	8.34%

Sensitivity Analysis in Forecasting Financial Statements

Impact of Changes in Selected Assumptions on Projected Income Statement
Colossal Chemical Corporation
Year Ended December 31, 2002
($000,000 omitted)

	Base Case	1% Increase in Gross Margin	1% Decline in Tax Rate	5% Increase in Sales
Sales	$2,110	$2,110	$2,110	$2,216
Cost of Goods Sold	1,161	1,139	1,161	1,219
Selling, General, and Administrative Expense	$ 528	$ 528	$ 528	$ 554
Depreciation	121	121	121	121
Research and Development	84	84	84	84
Total Costs and Expenses	1,893	1,872	1,893	1,977
Operating Income	$ 217	$ 238	$217	$ 238
Interest Expense	34	34	34	34
Interest (income)	–5	–5	–5	–5
Earnings before Income Taxes	$ 188	$ 209	$ 188	$ 209
Provision for Income Taxes	$ 64	$ 71	$ 62	$ 71
Net Income	$ 124	$ 138	$ 126	$138
Growth Sales	0%	0%	0%	5%
CGS as % of Sales	55%	54%	55%	55%
SG&A % of Sales	25%	25%	25%	25%
Taxrate	34%	34%	33%	34%

Impact of Changes in Selected Assumptions on Projected Income Statement
Colossal Chemical Corporation
Year Ended December 31, 2002
($000,000 omitted)

	Base Case	1% Increase in Gross Margin	1% Decline in Tax Rate	5% Increase in Sales
Sales	$2,110	$2,110	$2,110	$2,005
Cost of Goods Sold	1,161	1,118	1,161	1,102
Selling, General, and Administrative Expense	$ 528	$ 528	$ 528	$ 501
Depreciation	121	121	121	121
Research and Development	84	84	84	84
Total Costs and Expenses	1,893	1,851	1,893	1,809
Operating Income	$ 217	$ 259	$ 217	$ 196
Interest Expense	34	34	34	34
Interest (income)	–5	–5	–5	–5
Earnings before Income Taxes	$ 188	$ 230	$ 188	$ 167
Provision for Income Taxes	$ 64	$ 78	$ 62	$ 57
Net Income	$ 124	$ 152	$ 126	$ 110
Growth Sales	0%	0%		–5%
CGS as % of Sales	55%	53%	55%	55%
SG&A % of Sales	25%	25%	25%	25%
Taxrate	34%	34%	33%	34%

**Impact of Changes in Selected
Assumptions on Projected Income Statement
Colossal Chemical Corporation
Year Ended December 31, 2002
($000,000 omitted)**

		Base Case		Forecast
Sales		$2,110		$2,216
Cost of Goods Sold		1,161		1,174
Selling, General, and				
Administrative Expense		$ 528		$ 665
Depreciation		121		121
Research and Development		84		84
Total Costs and Expenses		1,893		2,044
Operating Income		$ 217		$ 172
Interest Expense		34		34
Interest (income)		−5		−5
Earnings before Income Taxes		$ 188		$ 143
Provision for Income Taxes		$ 64		$ 46
Net Income		$ 124		$ 97
Growth Sales			5%	
CGS as % of Sales	55%		53%	
SG&A % of Sales	25%		30%	
Taxrate	34%		32%	
Change in Sales Growth	5%			
Change in Gross Margin	−2%			
Change in SG&A % Sales	5%			
Taxrate	−2%			

Impact of Changes in Selected Assumptions on Projected Income Statement
Colossal Chemical Corporation
Year Ended December 31, 2002
($000,000 omitted)

	Base Case	1% Increase in Gross Margin	1% Decline in Tax Rate	5% Increase in Sales
Sales	$2,110	$2,110	$2,110	$2,216
Cost of Goods Sold	1,477	1,456	1,477	1,551
Selling, General, and Administrative Expense	$ 253	$ 253	$ 253	$ 266
Depreciation	121	121	121	121
Research and Development	84	84	84	84
Total Costs and Expenses	1,935	1,914	1,935	2,022
Operating Income	$ 175	$ 196	$ 175	$ 194
Interest Expense	34	34	34	34
Interest (income)	–5	–5	–5	–5
Earnings before Income Taxes	$ 146	$ 167	$ 146	$ 165
Provision for Income Taxes	$ 50	$ 57	$ 48	$ 56
Net Income	$ 96	$ 110	$ 98	$ 109
Growth Sales	0%	0%	0%	5%
CGS as % of Sales	70%	69%	70%	70%
SG&A % of Sales	12%	12%	12%	12%
Taxrate	34%	34%	33%	34%

Impact of Changes in Selected Assumptions on Projected Income Statement
Colossal Chemical Corporation
Year Ended December 31, 2002
($000,000 omitted)

	Base Case	2% Increase in Gross Margin	2% Decline in Tax Rate	5% Increase in Sales
Sales	$2,110	$2,110	$2,110	$2,216
Cost of Goods Sold	1,477	1,350	1,393	1,462
Selling, General, and Administrative Expense	$ 253	$ 317	$ 317	$ 332
Depreciation	121	121	121	121
Research and Development	84	84	84	84
Total Costs and Expenses	1,935	1,872	1,914	2,000
Operating Income	$ 175	$ 238	$ 196	$ 216
Interest Expense	34	34	34	34
Interest (income)	–5	–5	–5	–5
Earnings before Income Taxes	$ 146	$ 209	$ 167	$ 187
Provision for Income Taxes	$ 50	$ 71	$ 53	$ 64
Net Income	$ 96	$ 138	$ 113	$ 123
Growth Sales	0%	0%	0%	5%
CGS as % of Sales	70%	64%	66%	66%
SG&A % of Sales	12%	15%	15%	15%
Taxrate	34%	34%	32%	34%

**Impact of Changes in Selected
Assumptions on Projected Income Statement
Colossal Chemical Corporation
Year Ended December 31, 2002
($000,000 omitted)**

	Base Case		Forecast
Sales	$2,110		$2,216
Cost of Goods Sold	1,477		1,507
Selling, General, and			
Administrative Expense	$ 253		$ 377
Depreciation	121		121
Research and Development	84		84
Total Costs and Expenses	1,935		2,088
Operating Income	$ 175		$ 127
Interest Expense	34		34
Interest (income)	−5		−5
Earnings before Income Taxes	$ 146		$ 98
Provision for Income Taxes	$ 50		$ 31
Net Income	$ 96		$ 67
Growth Sales		5%	
CGS as % of Sales	70%	68%	
SG&A % of Sales	12%	17%	
Taxrate	34%	32%	
Change in Sales Growth	5%		
Change in Gross Margin	−2%		
Change in SG&A % Sales	5%		
Taxrate	−2%		